the
Abundance
diet

Grilled Eggplant and Zucchini Lasagna (page 174)

the
Abundance
diet

The 28-Day Plan
to Reinvent Your Health, Lose Weight,
and Discover the Power of Whole Foods

Somer McCowan

Foreword by Neal Barnard, M.D.

VEGAN HERITAGE PRESS
Woodstock • Virginia

ISBN 13: 978-1-941252-06-2
First Edition, June 2015
10 9 8 7 6 5 4 3 2 1

Vegan Heritage Press, LLC books are available at quantity discounts. For information, please visit our website at www.veganheritagepress.com or write the publisher at Vegan Heritage Press, P.O. Box 628, Woodstock, VA 22664-0628.

Library of Congress Cataloging-in-Publication Data

McCowan, Somer.
  The abundance diet : the 28-day plan to reinvent your health, lose weight, and discover the power of plant-based foods / Somer McCowan. — First edition.
    pages cm
  Includes bibliographical references and index.
  ISBN 978-1-941252-06-2 (paperback)
  1. Reducing diets—Recipes. 2. Vegan cooking—Recipes. 3. Cooking (Natural foods) 4. Weight loss. I. Title.
  RM222.2.M4336 2015
  641.5'636—dc23
                    2015002799

Cover Design: Annie Oliverio. **Photo credits:** Cover and interior food photography by Annie Oliverio. Incidental spot photos from stock photo sources. **Cover Photos:** (front) Cheesy Cauliflower Potato Bake, page 172; (back, from top) Vegetable Pudla, page 80; Raw Pad Thai, page 166; Cherry Garcia Soft-Serve, page 202.

Disclaimer: The information provided in this book should not be taken as medical advice. If you require a medical diagnosis or prescription, or if you are contemplating any major dietary change, juice fast, or change in your exercise habits, consult a qualified health-care provider. You should always seek an expert medical opinion before making changes in your diet or supplementation regimen. Neither the publisher nor the author are responsible for readers' health issues.

Publisher's Note: The information in this book is correct and complete to the best of our knowledge. Website addresses and contact information were correct at the time of publication. The publisher is not responsible for specific health or allergy issues or adverse reactions to recipes contained in this book.

Vegan Heritage Press books are distributed by Andrews McMeel Publishing.

Printed in the United States of America

Dedication

For my parents, Boni and Milo McCowan, who gave me my love of creating beautiful things in the kitchen and for teaching me that sharing a delicious meal with others is one of the best ways to open hearts and form lifelong friendships. Thank you for always opening your hearts, home, and kitchen to all those you know and love.

Niçoise Salad with Smoky Tofu and Creamy Miso Dressing (page 116)

Contents

Foreword

WHEN I FIRST LEARNED the name of Somer McCowan's book, *The Abundance Diet,* I thought it was perfect.

In the most literal sense, a low-fat vegan diet is abundant in that it allows you to eat plentiful amounts of food without having to limit portions, count carbohydrates or calories, or go hungry. For many people, this is a completely new experience. In the clinical research studies that we conduct here at the Physicians Committee, our participants are always amazed to learn that they don't need to restrict the amount that they eat. In fact, most people tell us that eating a low-fat vegan diet is easier than any other weight-loss or get-healthy strategy they've tried. Choosing the right foods and eating them in abundance is so much simpler, and more enjoyable, than counting calories or restricting portion sizes.

This is because plants provide an abundance of nutrition. If you're looking for the most nutrient-dense foods on the planet, plants always take home the gold. Full of fiber, vitamins, minerals, and phytonutrients, plants are nutritional powerhouses. Plants are also devoid of cholesterol and generally low in calories and saturated fat. Eating a plant-based diet increases the nutrient-density of your meals while lowering the calorie-density, which is the perfect equation for health.

Accordingly, a low-fat vegan diet brings an abundance of health benefits. We recently published a large meta-analysis in the *Journal of the Academy of Nutrition and Dietetics* showing that switching to a vegan diet leads to healthy weight loss—but this isn't news to anyone familiar with scientific research documenting the effects of plant-based diets. Studies consistently show that people who remove animal products from their diet are at a healthier weight than people who eat meat and dairy products (even when portions are larger). And the benefits don't stop there! Plant-based diets help people with diabetes to reduce their medications or in many cases, eliminate the need to take them altogether. This way of eating also tackles the roots of cardiovascular disease—reversing damage to the endothelial lining and opening up arteries to allow blood to flow smoothly throughout the body once again. And while you're losing weight and reversing your diabetes or heart disease, you can also lower blood pressure, reduce or eliminate pain from arthritis or migraines, protect your memory from Alzheimer's disease, increase energy, and much more. The health benefits you'll receive from one simple dietary pattern are abundant indeed, and quite astounding.

The abundance of benefits continues if we look to the environmental effects of our food choices. The meat industry produces more greenhouse gases than all worldwide transportation, in addition to fueling other environmental destruction. Thankfully, the fact that what we put on our plate can affect the health of the planet (in addition to our own health) is finally becoming well-known. The 2015 Dietary Guidelines Advisory Committee wrote, "The major findings regarding sustainable diets were that a diet higher in plant-based foods, such as vegetables, fruits, whole grains, legumes, nuts, and seeds, and lower in calories and animal based foods is more health promoting and is associated with less environmental impact than is the current U.S. diet." By removing animals and their by-products from our diets, we can play a significant role in reducing our environmental footprint and promoting a sustainable future.

Many people are also happy to know that by eating a vegan diet, they are saving the lives of millions of animals and practicing a more ethical lifestyle in this regard as well.

If you're wondering how to get started or how to make it work in your current lifestyle, Somer has created a wonderful step-by-step guide to help you get started. For now, just focus on the next four weeks. Read through this book and let Somer's expert advice help you to prepare, and then jump in—ALL in. Go for it, give it a try, and see what you think when the four weeks are up. Believe me, it will go by more quickly than you think, and you'll be delighted with your results!

Eat an abundance of plants and enjoy an abundance of benefits. You won't regret it!

—Neal Barnard, M.D.

Introduction

THE WORD "DIET" is typically associated with hunger, restriction, deprivation, calorie or points counting, meager portions, and special foods. In writing this book, I want to help people associate the word "diet" with its core meaning: the kinds of food that a person habitually eats. While following *The Abundance Diet,* you will not have to count calories, weigh your foods, add up points, or eat within certain hours. I've already done the work for you in planning and creating healthy, delicious, and nutritious recipes that will ensure weight-loss success.

To eat an "abundance diet" means you get to eat often and you get to eat serving sizes that are large enough to help you feel satisfied. Because whole-plant foods are naturally low in calories while providing complete nutrition, you don't have to worry about getting enough protein or balancing carbs and fats and other nutrients. You simply get to enjoy eating delicious food that happens to be very good for you. The food in my 28-Day Plan is whole, vegan, and naturally nutrient-dense and calorie-light. Plant foods are the best foods to give you the lifestyle that is full of abundance. So while this is indeed a diet book, it's important to understand how it differs from other diet books.

Since I myself went plant-based, I've read no fewer than 100 books on vegan living, most of which revolve around the health aspect of the diet. As a result, I've learned the right methods within my diet parameters for balancing my life, taking care of my body, and eating healthfully. After all, I once lost 100 pounds in less than a year without the help of anyone else (more on that story later). But even I've gotten off track from time to time, so over the last couple of years I formulated a plan for when my diet gets derailed. I originally called my plan "The Green Smoothie Challenge." However, the plan was so much more than just green smoothies that, even though the name stuck, it didn't fully describe the actual challenge.

When I first shared the plan through my blog, Vedged Out, people around the world took part in the weeklong quest to become healthier. The response was overwhelming and heartwarming. I heard success stories from my readers in nearly every state, as well as across the globe. Newspaper articles, prominent health websites, bloggers, and individuals have featured the challenge or commented on my site or emailed me their stories detailing their amazing results.

My original challenge was based on a seven-day clean eating plan, but some readers wanted to lose more weight or just loved the way their newfound diet made them feel, so they extended it for weeks and even months with amazing results. With this book, I've created an all-new 28-day challenge to help you get in shape and stay that way. This plan is for anyone who feels the need eat more healthfully, lose weight, stay healthy, get back into shape after illness or injury, and more. It's for omnivores, vegetarians, and vegans alike. *The Abundance Diet* is for you, whether you have started a healthy eating plan and want to continue to maintain it with a healthier twist; if you simply want to get ready for swimsuit season; or you need a cleanse after too much indulgent or holiday eating.

During the next 28 days, I'll help you eliminate processed foods, refined fats, sugars, and toxic foods. These foods will be replaced with whole plant foods and superfoods in abundance. You'll also be cutting out caffeine and alcohol consumption to allow you to regain your natural energy reserves. You will be eating more fiber on a daily basis then you probably did in a week on your previous diet. I promise: your colon and your heart will thank you!

Your daily meals will be rich with delicious green smoothies, hearty breakfast options, beautiful salads, healthy and filling main courses, tasty snacks, and special plant-based celebratory treats for the weekend. Healthy eating has never felt or tasted so good! Unless you have a mitigating metabolism or other disorder, you can eat 4 to 6 of the meals outlined in this book per day and still lose weight. The best part? I'm going to make it easy for you. While weight loss is almost exclusively about "calories in" versus "calories out," I've simplified the method so you don't have to count calories. Also, something magical happens when your diet consists entirely of whole plant foods: you lose weight at a more rapid and sustainable rate despite the number of calories consumed. Yes, I'm saying that 1,200 calories of whole plant foods behaves far better in your body than 1,200 calories of refined, processed, or animal foods. This book not only provides you with a concise 28-day diet plan, but also includes an optional bonus juice "feast" to kick-start your weight loss and/or health journey. The plan includes over 100 recipes and is customizable to suit your individual taste. All of these recipes are gluten-free to accommodate those with allergies or sensitivities to gluten.

If you're wondering whether this will all be worthwhile, participants in my original Green Smoothie Challenge typically lost 4 to 7 pounds in the first week, and in some cases more. One participant lost 17 pounds after three weeks on the challenge. I can't guarantee how much weight you'll lose—that will depend on your body composition, exercise level, and many other factors—but what I can tell you is this: the program is not a starvation or calorie-counting plan. So forget about points, put away your food-tracking system, eat nutritious plant foods to your heart's content, and you'll still lose weight. Results are typical!

My hope is that you'll develop new habits throughout this 28-day journey that will help you stick to cleaner eating patterns for life. Your health, your heart, your waistline, and the planet will be glad you did! If you are able to commit for the 28 days, I'm convinced that the results you achieve from following this plan will change the way you eat for life.

Don't forget that adding a healthy level of exercise to your regimen will help you reach these goals even faster. I've included a chapter on fitness for almost any fitness ability. Let's get started!

Part 1
Getting Started

ONE

My Personal Journey

I WAS A TEENAGER when I first flirted with vegetarianism. Many of my close friends were vegetarian, and it seemed like the cool thing to do. Unfortunately, to us teens the term "vegetarian" wasn't necessarily associated with healthy whole plant foods such as fresh produce, legumes, whole grains, nuts, and seeds. Instead, it meant we ate pink frosted sugar cookies and Doritos for lunch, washed down with a Coke. Clearly I didn't know the slightest thing about nutrition, or even why I was vegetarian—I was simply trying to be cool. But I maintained a vegetarian diet for a couple of years and began developing my love for cooking.

Fast forward a few years. I had met and married my husband in Australia, and we had moved to the United States. He was studying for his degree, and I was working full-time as an administrative assistant in a real estate office. Our diets were horrible, since we were eating as cheaply as possible on our limited budget. Ramen noodles and blue-box macaroni and cheese prevailed.

A few doors down from my office was a real estate agent named Denley Fowlke, a raw-food vegan. I had never even heard of raw as a diet choice. He was a picture of radiant health: lean and tanned, with perfect teeth and a glowing complexion. At the time, I was baffled that anyone could eat a diet consisting of raw vegetables, fruits, plants, sprouted grains, nuts, and seeds all the time! I didn't really get the issue with consuming meat, or the no-dairy aspect. Wasn't meat full of necessary protein? Wasn't milk full of calcium and good for your bones? Didn't it do a body good? While I hadn't yet figured out the answers to those questions about meat or dairy, the man had a profound influence on me.

On his suggestion, I tried my first juice fast. I even went out and bought what was then a top-of-the-line juicer—a Champion, which I still own and which still works like a champion. I went through a stint of trying to eat raw and vegan for nearly six months, but I threw in the towel when everything started to taste like grass. I was simply doing it wrong. I probably wasn't getting the right levels of nutrients. I didn't really have the tools or resources to have success, and I still didn't have the complete picture.

Later, my eating habits worsened and so did my health. After some high-stress life events, including multiple miscarriages, my health was at its all-time worst. At twenty-eight years of age, I was diagnosed with pre-cancer in my colon in addition to ulcerative colitis, a form of inflammatory bowel disease. This disease is marked by moderate to severe abdominal pain, bleeding from the bowels, and more. My physician removed the pre-cancerous cells and prescribed an arsenal of medications, including a very high dose of a corticosteroid called prednisone. While on the prednisone, I started to gain weight at a very rapid rate.

When I finally got to a point in my treatment where I could wean off the steroid, I had gained nearly 100 pounds over nine months. I asked my doctor if the weight would just come off, like water weight. He told me I would need to work off the weight, as if I had been eating massive cheeseburgers for the nine months I had been on the drug.

Up until this point, I had never been an especially physically fit or active person. Even when I was very slender, it just seemed to be good genes that kept me slim. Those good genes weren't going to help me lose the additional weight I was carrying, so I knew I had to do something more drastic in order to take control of my health and my body.

I joined a gym. It was one of the most humiliating experiences of my life, having to go to the gym and work out when I was the least fit I had ever been, but I knew I needed to get the weight off. I did one hour of cardio and one hour of weights nearly every day. I started counting calories as well, which was really quite awful, as anyone who's ever done so knows.

One year later, I had lost the 100 pounds and had run two half-marathons. Fitness-wise, I felt on top of the world. Unfortunately, despite the cardiovascular and muscle strength I had gained by running and lifting weights, my body was still in the throes of my disease, and I had no control over when it would strike. I would be training for a race and have to drop out because of an ugly flare-up.

I was put back on steroid prescription drugs over and over again, and continued to battle the weight gain. I really thought it would never end and that I would battle and suffer from my disease for life. At that time, I literally felt like garbage. I was sluggish and I had no energy.

Then, one weekend, my brother Abe asked me to watch the documentary Forks over Knives with him. I was astounded by the scientific facts about diet and health that were presented in the film by doctors and experts. The "test" subjects in the film experienced remarkable health changes and freedom from their ailments in an amazingly short period of time.

All of it just seemed to click and make sense to me. I realized that I might heal myself of the disease that had been plaguing me for nearly a decade simply by changing my diet. I thought it to be a ridiculously simple solution.

My husband and I agreed to experiment with a whole-foods plant-based diet as a family for thirty days, just to see how it would affect my health. Incredibly, just a couple of weeks into plant-based eating, I was able to come off all my medications. I can't express my relief at not having to continue to take those damaging drugs anymore.

Currently, I am completely off all prescription drugs, and my ulcerative colitis has been in full remission for more than three years since the inception of my whole-foods diet.

The only times I have experienced adverse stomach issues other than the occasional stomach bug were a few occasions in the early days of my plant-based journey when, at a restaurant, I accidentally consumed dairy. After each occasion, my body revolted. I learned to be more informed, ask more questions, and ask to see product labels when dining out to avoid making myself sick.

It is now very clear to me that animal products trigger my autoimmune disease and that, as long as I adhere to a clean vegan diet low in refined fats and sugars and high in nutrients, my disease will remain in remission.

I've loved the way I eat and how it makes my body feel, and I know my success is a direct result of eating vegan. It's amazing that the cure I was looking for comes from eating plants. I wish I had known years ago that I could heal my own body with what I was putting into my mouth.

Why a Plant-Based Diet Makes Sense

I realize that sometimes weight loss isn't enough to keep someone committed to a whole-foods plant-based diet, so I'd like to share information about some of the other important reasons to consider a vegan diet.

Mounting medical and scientific evidence supports the wisdom of a plant-based diet. Entire books and decades-long studies about the effects and side effects of producing and eating animal products have provided data that have become mainstream. Facts from these studies include the following:

- Eating meat significantly increases the odds of developing many types of cancer (Campbell, 2006).
- Populations who eat the least amount of meat have the longest and most disease-free lives (Fuhrman, 2013).
- Eating a plant-based diet can prevent and reverse heart disease (Esselstyn, 2008).
- Not only do vegans tend to be thinner and live longer than their meat-eating counterparts, but they also have significantly lower rates of diabetes, heart attacks, cancer and many other food- related diseases (www.adventisthealth-study.org).

A whole-foods vegan diet is not only the best diet for your body, it also happens to be the best diet for improving the health of our planet and reducing our environmental impact.

When You Make the Transition

It took me months to figure out how to eat an entirely plant-based diet after developing my meals mostly around meat for so much of my life. I've spent the last three years honing my skills in the kitchen to create food that is more delicious and nutritious than anything I ever ate before. In short, I have done all the work so that you can simply use the recipes in this book and start out with success in your own kitchen and skip the learning curve.

Shortly after I started blogging, the Forks Over Knives website featured a testimonial about my drastic health changes that I attributed to a whole-foods, plant-based diet. A couple of months later, ChooseVeg.org published my photo and story and included me in a brochure. I have been featured on the Food Network website as a vegan food expert. Many of my recipes are available on hugely popular websites or print publications, including OneGreenPlanet.org, Sunwarrior.com, ToneItUp.com, *Vegan Lifestyle Magazine,* and BuzzFeed.com, among other publications around the world. I have catered vegan events for 200-plus people and for smaller, more intimate gatherings. I receive thousands of hits daily on my website, VedgedOut.com, and I consult with people on a daily basis through social media about how to change their diets to regain health, lose weight, and eat incredibly delicious food.

I've helped people with all kinds of diets to improve their eating habits and their health. These include omnivores who have cut out most of the meat and dairy in their diets, vegetarians who have ditched milk and cheese, and even long-term vegans who have simply been eating too much processed vegan food and needed to get their diets back on track.

I believe that if you give the diet a try for just 28 days, your weight will begin to normalize, because plant-based foods can fill you up quickly without a calorie and fat overload. Your skin will look healthier and clearer because you are putting the right type of fuel in your body.

I also contend that you can start to reduce or eliminate symptoms from a variety of illnesses. When you provide your body with everything it needs to function well and heal itself, amazing things can happen. I can't wait to help you reach your goal.

Two

Your Relationship with Food

IT'S WELL KNOWN that many Americans are overweight. Attempting to lose weight, they try some form of Atkins- or Paleo-type diet and shun carbohydrates like they're evil. A high percentage of these people believe that even fruit is bad for them! Avoiding carbohydrates over the long term, of course, leads to yo-yo dieting, because avoiding carbohydrates forever just isn't sustainable. At the first reintroduction of them back into the diet, people balloon right back to their original weight, or worse.

Most people who need to lose weight typically face some sort of obstacle or barrier to reaching their goal because they have developed negative eating patterns. The key to your success with weight loss is identifying your particular barriers and then finding a solution for overcoming them. You can do this by developing one or more positive eating behaviors. (See the Positive and Negative Eating Patterns chart on page 9.)

Negative eating patterns can also be identified in more serious food behaviors, such as anorexia, binge eating, and food addiction. Binge eating is consuming unreasonable amounts of food in a short period of time. This type of eating isn't good for anyone, no matter what foods they are consuming. Binge eaters can sometimes eat the equivalent of two or more meals at one sitting, like an entire pizza, a two-liter bottle of soda, and a pint or more of ice cream.

Having a food addiction is no different than being addicted to drugs, cigarettes, alcohol, pornography, sex, gaming, shopping, or gambling. The end results are usually obesity and multiple health concerns. People who suffer from food addiction turn to food when they are bored, stressed, sad, angry, or tired. Other emotions can trigger the desire to eat as well, depending on the person and the severity of the addiction. Food addicts struggle in social settings, concerned that others will see them overeating and judge them. Therefore, it's not unusual for food addicts to eat in private. Severe food addicts may have secret stashes of high-calorie junk food and treats. Food addicts may not know that they are addicts or that they have a problem with addiction at all. They may just think they are wired differently, destined by genes to be overweight, or that they overeat simply because it makes them feel good.

It's important to take the next step in taking care of yourself by realizing that negative eating patterns can come from anywhere. Being raised in an environment where healthy food wasn't a priority, feeling overwhelmed by learning to cook healthy meals, loving the convenience of drive-thru and takeout food are all part of negative eating patterns. Food becomes like a comfort blanket, numbing heightened emotions and giving instant gratification.

Reversing Negative Eating Patterns

While you may not be able to change the stimuli of your negative eating pattern, you can reverse the trend by replacing the negative eating behavior with a positive one. Here are some trusted methods by which you can begin coping with whatever barriers you may be facing.

Exercise instead of eat. Sounds simple, right? Because many negative food patterns stem from eating triggered by boredom, stress, or other difficult emotions, it makes sense to throw exercise at those emotions rather than a doughnut. Exercise gives you happy endorphins, releases stress, and has an anti-depressive effect over time that is as powerful as taking a prescription anti-depressant, when done regularly. It also acts as an appetite suppressant rather than an appetite stimulant. Plus you get all the health benefits of working out, which can negate many of the negative feelings and issues associated with food addiction.

Make sure you are fully hydrated. That's right: drinking water, and lots of it, will help the body to feel fuller all the time. It's a simple trick. Reach for a glass of water before you reach for something else. Ten minutes after drinking the glass of water, evaluate whether you are really and truly hungry rather than just reacting to something. If you are, then go ahead and eat your next scheduled meal or snack.

Schedule your eating times. I advocate eating multiple times a day to ward off true hunger (you'll see later on in the book that eating more frequently doesn't necessarily mean eating smaller portions; I'm going to teach you to eat smarter, not make it harder with starvation tactics). For some people, eating times will occur every two hours, while others may need every three. Whatever you find works best for you, create that schedule and stick to it. You'll be much more likely to succeed if you're not worried about when you'll eat next.

Change your reward system. Do this for yourself and your family. Many people who struggle with their weight exhibit habits in which food is always the reward for accomplishments and achievements. I'm not saying that food can't be enjoyed, but why not reward yourself with a weekend away, a new outfit, or a spa visit instead of a calorie-laden meal?

Identify Your Positive and Negative Eating Patterns

Positive Eating means:

- eating when you are actually hungry.
- eating until you feel fulfilled but not overly stuffed.
- eating foods that you enjoy and that are nourishing to your body.
- eating as few as three meals a day or as many as six meals a day.
- not focusing on food all of the time.
- recognizing that while food is delicious, it's also meant to be used to fuel your body.

Negative Eating means:

- eating when you feel emotional, bored, or stressed, even if you don't feel hungry.
- often eating until you are stuffed to the point of feeling uncomfortable.
- feeling guilty about food and your body most of the time.
- skipping meals, or, alternatively, eating and grazing all day long.
- thinking about food all the time; food is a higher priority than many other needs or wants in your life.
- mostly eating foods that aren't nourishing. If you compare your body to a vehicle, it needs the right kind and right grade of fuel in order to run its best. Putting the wrong grade and wrong type of fuel in your body can lead to sluggishness, poor performance, and more.

Keep a food journal. Although it sounds cliché, this method really works! Simply write down absolutely everything that you eat in a day. Some days it will shock you. The best way to control a negative eating pattern is to eat with purpose and be aware of what you are eating. Documenting what you eat makes you more accountable to yourself and can keep you from negative eating.

Identify your feelings. This is important when you have urges to reach for something. Are you really hungry or are you just bored, tired, angry, or stressed? Most often, I think you will find that, apart from scheduled mealtimes, you are reaching for a snack because you are feeling boredom or some other emotion and you are trying to squelch it with food that you do not truly need. If you can identify the emotion, then you can do something else about it such as filling your time with productive things instead of just snacking.

Learn to love yourself. Loving yourself and your body will help you achieve your ideal weight more effectively than all of these other tips combined. Realize you've got a body that can move and is beautiful no matter what the shape or size. Use positive self-talk. What might feel cheesy in the beginning, like giving yourself a compliment about a feature or a quality you have, will start to feel more natural as you practice it. Don't say negative things about yourself, as it reinforces these thoughts. Instead, radiate happiness and positive thoughts, and you will feel more physically attractive, you will be less down, and you will be better able to use that goodness to brighten the lives of others as well.

You may have days where you don't particularly like your shape or the number on the scale, but that's no reason to berate yourself or treat your body poorly by eating un-

healthy foods. Eat mindfully with food that nourishes and heals the body, take the time to savor it, and appreciate that you can put healthy food on the table.

Does that mean you can't have a treat or special occasion meal? Certainly not. If you condemn yourself to a life where you can't celebrate and enjoy food, then life gets a little more barren. Once you've got a handle on things, you'll be better at practicing moderation. It really is okay to eat a vegan cupcake or cookie once in a while or a meal that is more rich than you would occasionally make at home. Just treat those events as they are: special occasions. For the most part, you should choose not to keep treats or junk food in your house if possible, because if it is there, it's likely you will end up eating it without a special purpose. You want to create a foundation of healthy eating habits that can sustain you in the long run. I'll be here to help.

Luckily, *The Abundance Diet* recipes are based entirely on plant foods that are full of fiber and which fill you up more quickly than foods that don't contain any fiber, namely, animal foods. Also, plant foods generally contain fewer calories than animal foods and contain many more nutrients. This is why plants are so great at helping to control appetite! If, in addition to your main daily dinner course, you are eating plenty of salads, whole grains, fruits, vegetables, nuts, and seeds in moderation, then you are more likely to reach your healthy weight and maintain it.

THREE

Reinventing Your Kitchen

IF YOU ARE READY to get the unhealthy foods out of your house and the clean foods in, this chapter is important for your success. I'll walk you through the steps and help you get your kitchen into plant-based shape in no time.

The first thing to do is completely clean out your fridge, freezer, and pantry. That's right; remove every item that is overly processed or that could be defined as junk food. This cleanup will even include foods that are technically vegan but that are processed or fried, like Oreos, corn chips, and potato chips. Just because a food is vegan doesn't mean it's healthy for you or that you should have it in your home where you might feel tempted to eat it just because it is available. If you keep tempting, unhealthy foods around, I guarantee you'll end up eating them and sabotaging your best efforts at better health. If your fridge and pantry are full of good and wholesome foods, then your body will be as well. That's where your transformation begins.

I'm not telling you that you can never consume anything unhealthy again, just that junk foods or processed foods should be considered as very limited celebration foods, as in a few times a year and not every weekend. In time, I think you'll find that they've become too sweet and junky for you to enjoy. You'll find that smaller portions will suffice or that healthier replacements will replace the bad foods you once loved.

Now, this full-scale kitchen clean-out obviously encompasses a lot of different types of food (or non-food), so I'm going to help you out. Remove from your home any items that contain:

- white sugar
- white flour
- artificial colorings or flavorings
- ingredients that you can't recognize or whose sources you don't understand
- anything with trans-fats or that is hydrogenated
- anything with more than a dozen "real" ingredients

Artificial, processed and refined foods are harmful to your health and your waistline. Remember, you only want to keep real, whole, plant-based foods in your home.

Next, you are going to get rid of everything in your fridge and pantry that contains animal products of any kind. Some obvious things you'll be removing from your home are milk, ice cream, cheese, butter, eggs, beef, chicken, pork, bacon, processed luncheon meats, and any other kind of food that comes directly from an animal. For some of the sneakier ingredients, you'll have to read labels. Watch out for ingredients such as gelatin, lactose, lard, whey, casein, egg albumin, natural chicken or beef flavor, carmine (a red food coloring that comes from crushed beetles), rennet, tallow, chicken fat, collagen, elastin, and anything else that may be obvious to you. Of course there are many more hidden animal ingredients, but by their nature they're harder to find. Go with ingredients you can pronounce and recognize, and you'll be safe.

Vegans, make sure to clean out any vegan foods masquerading as health foods, including vegan cookies and crackers and processed vegan meats, cheeses, and ice creams. Just because they are vegan doesn't make them health foods. It's easy to fall into a trap of buying products simply because they are vegan.

You may be surprised how many items start stacking up. I certainly was the first time I cleaned out my pantry. Try not to stress about the items going out; some of them aren't real food anyway, so you shouldn't be putting those items into your body. You've also got to realize that while you are "de-junking" your kitchen, you are making an investment in your health.

Here's the part where you get to feel like a saint. I want you to donate all of your non-perishable items in the "no-no pile" to your local food bank. As many as one in five Americans go hungry every day. If you've skipped lunch here or there on a busy day, that's not the same as coming home and having nothing to eat and no funds to buy the food you need to live. You can help sustain the lives of others while you are on the quest to improve your health. Such items can also be donated to your local place of worship. The point is, if you don't have it in your house, you're not going to be tempted to eat it! I promise, getting rid of that pile will make the transition a whole lot easier.

When you follow the shopping lists I provide in the book, you'll be filling your shopping cart with vegetables, fruits, whole grains, nuts, seeds, beans, and non-dairy milk. I mostly use homemade unsweetened almond milk in this book, but if you have an allergy to almonds, you can certainly use other delicious plant milks, which include those made with soy, coconut, rice, cashew, hemp, oat, flax, and more. For health purposes, it's best to go with light or unsweetened varieties rather than the sweetened, full-fat varieties.

To Save Money

I recommend saving money through bulk bin shopping at your local health food store. The bulk bin prices are sometimes what you'd pay for an item on the shelf, and the foods are just as fresh and nutritious.

I have a membership at Costco, where I buy giant bags of organic kale, spinach, and frozen fruit; inexpensive bananas; and bulk items for other things we use often. If you have a similar membership, use it. You don't have to make all the smoothies in this book. Just buy a few large bags of single fruit or mixed fruit that you enjoy. Doing this saves me lots of

money on produce, even over other big box stores. If you are worried about the food spoiling before you can use it all, freeze it. Extra spinach, kale, and bananas can go straight into your freezer. Freezing these items straight away stops any browning or wilting and wasted produce. Nutrient loss with frozen food is minimal, so you'll always have nutritious ingredients on hand to prepare your smoothies. Freezing also means you won't have to run to the store as often.

I also recommend supporting your local farmer's market or CSA (Community Sustained Agriculture), where you can scour for good deals or slightly bruised seconds. If you can get a box of inexpensive peaches or other favorite fruits, chop them up, freeze them, and use them in your smoothies!

To get you started, below are six basic recipes to have on hand to make cooking *The Abundance Diet* way easier.

Six Basic Recipes

I want to introduce a few recipes that, if you make some up in advance, you can use throughout the book. It's best to keep a batch of each in the fridge so you've got them ready to use. For those who prefer not to use tofu, I'm also providing a recipe for Burmese Tofu, a tofu-like ingredient that contains no soy.

Somer's All-Purpose Gluten-Free Flour Blend

I was trying recipes with only one or two gluten-free flours, but I wasn't having very good results. This is the blend I came up with for light and fluffy baked goods. It has a very similar flavor and texture to whole wheat pastry flour. If you'd like, you can use a store-bought blend of gluten-free flours in your recipes, but make sure to use one that has mostly whole grains in the ingredient list.

- **1 cup superfine ground almond flour**
- **1 cup oat flour (from certified gluten-free oats)**
- **1 cup tapioca starch**
- **1 cup sorghum flour**

Combine all the ingredients in a large Ziploc bag. Shake until well mixed. Store in the refrigerator or freezer for freshness.

MAKES 4 CUPS

Notes: If you have a high-speed blender, you can grind your own almond and oat flours to save money, but the end result will be slightly grainier than the commercial versions.

If you have oat allergies, use millet flour instead of oat flour. If you have almond allergies, use coconut flour instead of almond flour.

Easiest Plant Milks

These plant milks are great in smoothies or for pouring over oats, muesli, or cold cereal. They can also be used for cooking in place of dairy milk.

> **2 tablespoons unsweetened raw or roasted almond butter, cashew butter, coconut butter, or sunflower seed butter**
> **3 cups water**

Combine the nut butter and water in your blender and blend until thoroughly emulsified.

Transfer to a lidded mason jar and refrigerate.

This will keep refrigerated for 3 to 4 days. Shake before using, because homemade plant milk can and does separate. If you find separation annoying, add 1/8 teaspoon of guar gum to your plant milk to keep the mixture homogenized and add a thicker creamier texture.

Optional add-ins: a tiny pinch of sea salt or a half teaspoon of pure vanilla extract.

MAKES 3 CUPS

Cashew Cream

Use this recipe to add creaminess and to mimic dairy. You can use it to brighten soups, to drizzle over main courses, and even as simple salad dressing. If you can acquire vegan probiotic powder, a half teaspoon can be added to the batch during blending to increase storage life and nutrient content.

> **1 cup raw cashew pieces (cashew pieces are less expensive than whole cashews)**
> **2 cups water**

Combine the cashews and water in your blender and blend until thoroughly emulsified. Transfer to a lidded mason jar and refrigerate.

This will keep refrigerated for 4 to 7 days. Shake before using.

MAKES 2 1/2 CUPS

Note: If you do not have a high-speed blender like a Blendtec or Vitamix, soak cashews in water to cover for 4 to 6 hours, then drain and rinse them before blending with fresh water.

Date Paste

This recipe is essential for the dessert recipes and many salad dressings in this book.

- **1 cup pitted dates**
- **2 cups warm water**

In a glass container or bowl, combine the dates and water. Cover the container and let the dates soak for 4 to 6 hours. Once the dates are soft and plump, transfer the dates in their liquid to a blender and blend until smooth and creamy.

Store the date paste in a lidded mason jar.

This will keep refrigerated for 7 to 10 days. Shake before using if necessary.

MAKES 2 1/2 CUPS

Note: A shortcut recipe is to combine date sugar (made from ground dried dates) with warm water, stirring until it is a paste consistency as needed for your recipe.

Fresh Vegan Mozarella

This vegan cheese stays "melted" until baked, when it forms a nice golden crust, like dairy cheese. I use it in this book to make the Cheesy Herb and Vegetable Crust Pizza on page 168, the Chiles Rellenos Casserole Bake on page 170, and the Grilled Eggplant and Zucchini Lasagna on page 174.

- **1/4 cup raw cashews (soaked for 4 to 6 hours)**
- **1 cup hot water**
- **2 tablespoons plus 1 teaspoon tapioca starch**
- **1 tablespoon nutritional yeast**
- **1 small garlic clove, minced**
- **1/2 teaspoon sea salt**
- **1 teaspoon fresh lemon juice**

In a blender, combine the cashews, water, tapioca starch, nutritional yeast, garlic, salt, and lemon juice. Blend until completely smooth, 1 to 2 minutes. Pour the cheesy sauce into a small saucepan and cook, stirring constantly with a wooden spoon, over medium-high heat.

After a couple of minutes, the mixture will start to look like it's curdling or separating. This is totally normal. Reduce heat to medium and keep stirring so it doesn't burn to the bottom of the pan. Keep cooking and stirring until the cheese is very thick, 2 to 3 more minutes. The mixture will become like a cohesive mass of melted dairy cheese and stretchy like a real cheesy sauce. Remove the Moxarella from the heat and let cool a bit before using.

Burmese Tofu

I use a lot of tofu in this book, so I wanted to provide an option for those who are soy-free. Use this as a soy tofu replacement for any recipe in the book calling for tofu, including stir fries, tofu scrambles, salad dressings, and desserts. Traditional Burmese tofu is not made from bean curd like the familiar soy-based Chinese and Japanese tofu. It's made from chickpea flour which is soaked in water for hours; then the water is skimmed off the top and the mixture is cooked. My method is faster and easier: your Burmese Tofu will be ready to use in about one hour. It doesn't have the same porosity as soy tofu, so you can't marinate it very well without its breaking down; however, you can add seasonings directly to the batter, remembering to reduce the amount of water in the recipe for any liquid you are replacing. You can pan-fry it or bake it and use it anywhere you would use regular firm tofu.

FOR FIRM BURMESE TOFU
1 cup chickpea flour
1 3/4 cups cold water

FOR SILKEN BURMESE TOFU
1/2 cup chickpea flour
1 1/3 cups cold water

Lightly oil a small rectangular or square dish (a tofu-sized container) and set it aside. In a small saucepan, whisk together the chickpea flour with the cold water until completely smooth. Heat over medium heat and stir constantly with a wooden spoon or heat-proof silicone spatula until very thick, about 5 minutes. Pour the tofu immediately into the prepared container and let set at room temperature and cool for one hour. Use now or cover and refrigerate for later use.

Burmese Tofu will keep for 5 to 6 days. If you plan to use it often, these recipes can be doubled or tripled (just remember to adjust the size of your container).

Note: for savory dishes, a 1/4 to 1/2 teaspoon of sea salt can be added to the batter.

Plant-Based Ingredients to Know and Love

Most of the ingredients used in this book are readily found in most supermarkets. Still, there may be a few that are new to you, so I've included them here. If you can't find these ingredients in a supermarket or natural foods store, they can be easily purchased online.

- *Nutritional yeast:* While not the same as bread yeast, this wonderful and flavorful food supplement is loved by vegans for its cheesy and savory flavor. Nutritional yeast is most affordable when purchased at a health food store in bulk bins, but it can also be ordered online. Just make sure that the brand you buy is fortified with vitamin B12 (most are).

- *Vegetable bouillon or quality vegetable broth:* I use broth in all my soup recipes instead of water as it imparts a bolder, heartier flavor. Use caution when you buy prepared vegetable broths and bouillon cubes because some brands contain sugar, hydrogenated oils, and MSG. You want to go for a clean label, and my personal favorite is Better Than Bouillon's Vegetable Base. It's a vegetable broth paste that you can find in well-stocked grocery stores or online. Make sure the label is vegan, and if you can get it, also organic. Use the instructions on the label to make up your liquid broth for recipes. For some of my recipes I prefer their No-Beef or No Chicken Base (both vegan). I also like the following brands of vegetable bouillon cubes: Edward and Sons, Rapunzel, and Massel.

- *Bragg Liquid Aminos or tamari:* I use Bragg Liquid Aminos as a seasoning almost on a daily basis, often to replace salt. It's a soy sauce alternative that's gluten-free and preservative-free. If you aren't able to find it and don't have issues with gluten, regular soy sauce can certainly be used in these recipes. You could also substitute tamari, which is a lovely soy sauce replacement. In most of my recipes, tamari and Bragg Liquid Aminos are interchangeable. Those with soy allergies can use coconut aminos instead of Bragg or tamari. Coconut aminos have less sodium than Braggs or tamari, so adjust the sodium in your recipes accordingly.

- *Stevia:* The sweet-tasting leaves of this South American plant are extracted and used as a sweetener and sugar substitute. Stevia is calorie-free and doesn't affect blood sugar levels, and it can be found in almost any grocery store in the sweetener section. If possible, look for versions without any additives. My favorite stevia is made by Nu-Naturals. I use it in all my smoothies, since the sweetness allows me to pack more greens into them. I use both liquid and powdered stevia in this book, so having both on hand will be helpful. If you are sensitive to stevia or don't enjoy it, try using one of these alternative low-calorie sweeteners instead: monk fruit, tagatose, lo han, xylitol, or erythritol. Some of these options have more calories than stevia, but are all low in calories compared to sugar, pure maple syrup, or agave. I haven't tested these recipes with anything but stevia, so use your favorite alternative to taste.

- *Miso:* Typically made from brown rice and soy, this Japanese fermented paste has a lovely pungent flavor and aroma that add a nice umami element to the recipes I use it in. If you have soy allergies, you can source miso made from chickpeas. For all of the recipes in this book, I use mellow white miso. You should be able to find it at any health food store. Chickpea miso can be purchased online.

- *Tapioca starch:* Also called tapioca flour, this starch comes from the cassava root. I use it to give cheesy foods a realistic stretch. I also use it as an ingredient in my gluten-free flour. Tapioca starch can typically be found in the gluten-free section of your grocery store or online. Cornstarch or arrowroot can be used instead of tapioca starch, but results will differ slightly as each has varying thickening abilities.

- *Plant milks:* For most of the recipes in this book I use unsweetened soy or almond milk. You can use whichever plant milk you prefer, or you can make homemade plant milk with the recipe above. Keep in mind that unsweetened plant milks are best.

- *Garbanzo or chickpea flour:* Also known as besan gram in Indian markets, this flour is made from ground dried garbanzo beans. I love the versatility of this ingredient. It can be used to replace eggs or create delicious gluten-free dishes. It is healthful, full of protein and fiber. You can find this ingredient at your health food store, online, or at an Indian grocer. I like Bob's Red Mill brand.

A Word About Food Allergies

The purpose of this book is to help you as much as possible in the kitchen to enjoy plant-based eating. If you have a food allergy, there are substitutions available for nearly any offending ingredient. I've listed the most common replacements below.

For allergies to cashews, almonds, and other tree nuts: I use tree nuts frequently in this book, but they can be replaced with an equal amount of raw pine nuts, hemp seeds, or sunflower seeds. They can also be replaced with half the amount of almond butter (if there isn't an allergy to almonds) or Sunbutter (sunflower butter). This means that, if the recipe calls for 1/2 cup cashews, you can replace that amount with 1/4 cup of almond butter or Sunbutter. The recipe will take on the slight flavor of whatever you are replacing the cashews with, but you should still end up with delicious results.

For soy allergies: Bragg Liquid Aminos or tamari are used in many recipes in this book. Both are made from soybeans. If you have a soy allergy, you can simply substitute coconut aminos in these recipes. Coconut aminos are lower in sodium than Bragg or tamari so you may have to taste and adjust the salt in the finished recipe as necessary. For recipes which call for tofu, you can use hemp tofu found at your health food store or Burmese Tofu (page 17) to replace the tofu in nearly every case.

For gluten allergies: Every recipe in this book is gluten-free. However, if you do have a gluten allergy or sensitivity, please take extra care to read all labels of food that you purchase to be sure that there is no hidden gluten.

For corn allergies: I use corn in just a few places in this book, including whole corn and non-GMO cornstarch in a few recipes. Replace whole corn with your favorite vegetable instead. Replace cornstarch with an equal amount of arrowroot or tapioca starch. Results may differ slightly, but not enough to negatively impact a recipe.

Finally, make an investment in your plant-based education. If you fully understand why you are going plant-based and have the tools and recipes to be successful, you will be less likely to give up or make errors. If you think it's too expensive to get educated and eat plant-based, consider the cost of cancer, prescription drugs for autoimmune illnesses, or a quadruple bypass. Here are some documentary films that I recommend: *Forks Over Knives, Vegucated, Chow Down,* and *Fat, Sick and Nearly Dead.* As of this writing, most of these films are available for streaming on Netflix, Hulu, or, for a small fee, on Amazon Instant Viewer.

Part 2
The 28-Day Plan

FOUR

Simplify Your Menu

WITHOUT A DOUBT, eating a healthy and clean diet takes a bigger investment of your time and mental energy than eating out or buying prepared and frozen meals at the grocery store. If you want to get on the right track, you have to make a commitment to a better diet. It takes a little work on your part, but in this chapter I'll teach you how you can save time in the kitchen, stretch your grocery dollars further, and prevent food waste.

I know how difficult it is in this busy world to find additional time, but everyone has the same twenty-four hours. How you spend those hours depends on where your priorities lie.

Consider that the average American spends about five hours a day watching television. Americans with smart phones or other digital devices spend another additional five hours a day online, on social media, and texting. With favorite TV shows to watch, e-mail to check, blogs to read, texts, and a host of social media, most of us waste a lot of time.

I'm not saying that you have to give up any of the above things, but if you spend over ten hours a day attached to your computer, smartphone, or TV, you can most definitely set aside time for healthy living. That being said, I want to provide you with the very best tools possible to help make the process easier, so you can succeed with your health and weight goals and get the results you want.

Saving Time in the Kitchen

With the exceptions of canned beans, tofu, store-bought pasta, and a few other necessities, every recipe in this book is prepared from scratch. The reason for this is that prepackaged foods are often processed and unhealthy. They contain chemicals, preservatives, artificial flavorings, and more. In addition, pre-packaged foods are more generally costly than homemade.

Generally, preparing meals from scratch requires some planning and time commitment. If you already prepare most of your meals at home and eat a lot of whole foods, pat yourself on the back. You've got this; the transition to this diet for you should be a snap. However, I think you'll still find some useful tips and timesaving tricks here.

If you mostly buy prepackaged foods or eat out more than you eat at home, this section is designed to make your life easier. Don't fret; it's simpler than it sounds. I have lots of shortcuts up my sleeve to help you streamline the process. Let's begin with some of my favorite time-saving kitchen tools that will help speed up cooking time and decrease stress.

Tools of the Trade

To make my recipes easily, your kitchen should be equipped with the following items:

- **A good cutting board.** Wood, glass, or plastic cutting boards work fine. If you are using plastic, try to ensure that your board is BPA-free. (Bonus: when you don't have any animal products in your house, you don't have to worry about food cross-contamination.)

- **A set of sharp kitchen knives.** Sharper knives, surprisingly, lead to fewer kitchen injuries, since blunt knives can skip off the surface of the items they are cutting. If your knives are dull, look into a knife sharpening system or consider getting your knives professionally sharpened.

- **A dozen or so lidded pint, cup, and quart mason jars.** These wonder jars are handy for storing smoothies, juices, soups, hummus, almond milk, and more. When a jar is filled to capacity and then lidded, foods are less likely to oxidize or lose nutrient value. Also, glass jars are naturally BPA- and hormone-free, unlike their plastic counterparts. These jars can be found online or at most big box stores.

- **A blender.** A high-speed, high-end blender, like those made by Blendtec or Vitamix, will work best for the recipes in this book. High-speed blenders make quick work of pureeing smoothies, grinding flax seeds, and preparing hummus, salad dressings, dips, salsa, sauces, and so much more. A lot of recipes in this book call for cashew cream, and blending cashews in a high-speed blender to smooth and creamy perfection is a cinch. I own a Blendtec, and it is my most loved and most used kitchen appliance. If you're wondering whether a high-speed blender is a worthwhile investment, consider this: before purchasing my Blendtec, I burned out the motors in no less than eight standard blenders. If you have burned out multiple blenders like I have, and a high-speed blender is within your budget, I highly recommend it. A regular blender can be used for most of these recipes provided that you have enough time for pre-soaking or defrosting your ingredients, but your results may not be as smooth or creamy as mine and will take longer to blend. For those of you with a smaller blender, such as Magic Bullet or Nutri-Bullet, some recipes may need to be prepared in batches to avoid blender overflow.

- **A food processor.** This is an indispensable multi-tasking kitchen gadget that slices, dices, cuts, shreds, blends, and chops. It can also make purees, pesto, nut butters, seed butters, and so much more. Food processors are also typically a breeze to clean up. Use them to shred carrots, cabbage, and kale for salads, to slice tomatoes, cucumbers, onions, zucchini, and more. Typically, precut vegetables will keep for up to three days when refrigerated, so prepare enough to last you for a few days when you have the food processor out and put whatever you are not using immediately into containers for later use. You can also use your food processor to make hummus, the fantastic desserts in my desserts chapter, and so much more.

- **A set of sturdy pots and pans including a proper nonstick skillet.** There are many varieties now that are environmentally safe and don't have toxins or contaminants in the nonstick layer. The one in my kitchen is a 12-inch Bialetti ceramic nonstick pan.

- **A juicer.** Get one if you plan on including the optional bonus juice feast. I have both a higher-end old-school Champion masticating juicer and a lower-end Hamilton Beach Big Mouth Pro centrifugal juicer. Masticating juicers are better at preserving the nutrients in the juice; Centrifugal juicers are better for speedy juicing. I love both of my juicers and use them frequently. Either variety or anything in between will work well for your juice feast. Those with centrifugal juicers may want to divide juice recipes into smaller batches and juice more often to preserve the nutrient integrity of your fresh juices.

- **Mandoline.** Rather than chopping on a work surface for ages, you can use a mandoline to cut vegetables and fruits quickly and efficiently. This tool also allows for a nice food presentation, as all of the slices will be uniform. I like using this tool while preparing salads, soups, and stews.

- **Other handy items.** These include baking dishes and baking sheets, a garlic press, a vegetable peeler, a micro-plane, a can opener, and essentials such as spatulas and wire whisks.

Slow Cookers

Every kitchen should have either a slow cooker or a pressure cooker, as they save time on busy days. You don't necessarily need both, so read on to decide which one is best for you.

Slow cookers are great for when you have a bit of time in the morning to get dinner underway. It's wonderful to come home from work, running errands, or being out all day and have a fragrant dinner bubbling and ready to serve. You simply add the ingredients to the pot in the morning, turn it on, and walk away. You can also cook ingredients in a slow cooker overnight while you sleep.

Slow cookers typically have multiple heat settings, including low, medium, and high, as well as a keep-warm feature. Higher-tech slow cookers may also have timers, sauté functions, and more. They are ideal for preparing all of the soups and stews in this book and some of the main course meals such as the casseroles. They are also great for cooking up quantities of brown rice, dried beans, lentils, "baked" potatoes, and many more food staples called for in this book. Those staples can be cooked in bulk, then frozen or refrigerated for later use. I freeze rice in one-cup portions and beans in 1 1/2 cup portions to make them easy to defrost and use in recipes.

There are many different sizes of slow cookers, so decide which one is right for you based on the size of your household. Singles and couples may want a smaller 2-quart slow cooker, while families will benefit from a larger, 4- or 6-quart capacity. To adapt recipes featured here in this book, refer to your slow cooker manual and use the times recommended for similar recipes provided to you by the manufacturer.

Pressure Cookers

Pressure cookers are the opposite of slow cookers in that they cook food quickly. There are lots of varieties, including stove top and electric models, though an electric model is the easiest one for beginners to use, since you can basically set it and forget it. You can come home from work, add the ingredients for your recipe, and have dinner on the table in less than half an hour, all with the push of a button. They are a "faster than picking up takeout" miracle. Pressure cookers can also be used similarly to slow cookers for batch-cooking rice, dry beans, lentils, potatoes, and more. The soups, stews, and casseroles in the Main Courses chapter can also be prepared in a pressure cooker. To adapt recipes featured here in this book, use the times recommended in your pressure cooker manual.

My pressure cooker is the energy-efficient Instant Pot 7-in-1 Programmable model. It's a pressure cooker, slow cooker, rice cooker, yogurt maker, steamer, and warmer all in one. It can even be used for sautéing and browning. It has a large stainless steel inner pot and an easy-to-use control panel with all the functions you could possibly need. Right now, aside from my Blendtec blender, it is my most used and best time-saving kitchen appliance.

If You Are on a Strict Budget

Kitchen items used in this book do not have to be high-end or even brand new. Many of the kitchen appliances I currently own have been purchased second-hand (and then well cleaned) through places like the Salvation Army or a local thrift store. You could also look in your local classifieds. Friends or family members may have an extra set or appliance that they would be willing to let you borrow until you can afford to set up your kitchen the way you wish. Items can also be purchased cheaply through big box stores during sales or ads.

Helpful Methods

Now that you've got an idea of tools that can save you time and money in the kitchen, let's talk about what methods you can use to get healthy meals on the table fast.

Having a meal plan is one of the single most effective time savers I use. Without a weekly plan, it seems like my kitchen time and mental state are far more chaotic. If you know exactly what you plan to eat and what you plan to shop for, you don't have to spend ages thinking of what to make each day or wander the grocery aisles aimlessly trying to figure out what to purchase. In the next chapter, I provide meal-planning tools and shopping lists, and ways to adapt the plan to fit your tastes, needs, and schedule.

"Eat-on-Repeat" is a term I use around my house for purposefully creating leftovers. Eating on repeat can make your life so much easier and help you save money on groceries since you aren't buying ingredients for a different meal for every single day of the week. It takes a little extra planning to decide when you are going to prepare your meals, but you end up spending less total time in the kitchen.

Double Up on Meal Prep

I like doing a lot of my meal prep on Sundays and again midweek. I often make a double or triple batch of soups, main courses, and salad dressings, so that I have extra on hand for meals later in the week.

Meals that will be eaten within the next few days get refrigerated, and anything intended to be eaten beyond the three day mark gets frozen. Most recipes in this book will keep well refrigerated for a few days, and most items can be frozen, with the exception of salads and smoothies. Salads and smoothies, of course, are prepared fresh each day, but generally they aren't time-consuming to prepare. Vegetables can be precut and stored, and smoothies can be bagged and ready to go. Purchasing the ingredients to make similar meals throughout the week also cuts down on grocery waste. So, by "eating on repeat," you can create a meal plan designed after repeats that look something like this:

When planning a menu for the week, include the following:

- 2 to 3 different smoothies
- 1 to 2 breakfasts
- 3 salads
- 3 soups
- 3 main courses
- 3 snacks
- 2 desserts

Your weekly meal plan will end up looking something like this:

A One-Week Sample Menu

Meal	Monday	Tuesday	Wednesday	Thursday	Friday	Saturday	Sunday
Smoothie / Breakfast	Annie's Da Cherry Bomb Smoothie	Mango Madness Green Smoothie	Green Julius	Annie's Da Cherry Bomb Smoothie	Mango Madness Green Smoothie	Carrot Cake Waffles	Quinoa Berry Banana Bowls
Salad	Green Goddess Spinach Salad	Delicious Curried Brown Rice Salad	Vegan Nicoise Salad	Green Goddess Spinach Salad	Delicious Curried Brown Rice Salad	Vegan Nicoise Salad	Green Goddess Spinach Salad
Soup	Cheesiest Potato Soup	Cozy Roasted Butternut Soup	Lightened Up African Peanut Stew	Cheesiest Potato Soup	Cozy Roasted Butternut Soup	Lightened Up African Peanut Stew	Cheesiest Potato Soup
Snack	Baked Nacho Cheesy Kale Chips	Oil-Free Hummus with Fresh Cut Vegetables	Cheesy Gluten-Free Crackers	Baked Nacho Cheesy Kale Chips	Oil-Free Hummus with Fresh Cut Vegetables	Cheesy Gluten-Free Crackers	Baked Nacho Cheesy Kale Chips
Main	Chili Relleno Casserole Bake	Grilled Eggplant and Zucchini Lasagna	Homestyle Mexican Casserole	Chili Relleno Casserole Bake	Grilled Eggplant and Zucchini Lasagna	Homestyle Mexican Casserole	Chili Relleno Casserole Bake
Dessert	none	none	none	none	none	Chocolate Orange Silk Mousse	Luscious Creamy Lemon Tarts

Examples of complete meal plans and shopping lists are provided in the next chapter. Of course, you can create your own meal plans and shopping lists following the same idea, or if you aren't a leftovers person, you can make your meals fresh every day as you go.

Saving Money

People often ask me if a vegan diet is more expensive than a regular diet. The truth is, there are lots of different answers to that question. Most likely, you can reduce your grocery budget by going vegan. But, like with any diet, it really depends on what you are purchasing at the grocery store. The average family of four spends typically spends anywhere from $146 to $289 a week on groceries. Obviously, there are vegan, omnivore, and mixed families that spend less or more than those amounts, depending on their circumstances, food choices, and budget.

A produce-rich diet such as *The Abundance Diet* can definitely be kept within the above budget parameters, but may seem slightly more expensive if you are not used to purchasing lots of fresh ingredients, or if you spend most of your dining dollars eating out on the dollar menu instead of purchasing items to make meals at home. Indeed, one organic apple can cost more than a double cheeseburger on a fast-food dollar menu. If this is the case, be sure to consider that you are getting a much higher quality nutrient value per dollar than if you were eating less produce or more restaurant food.

I love shopping at my local health food store or fancy natural market more than any other place, but when I'm on a budget, I stick to those stores for specialty items only. I use a Costco wholesale membership to purchase bulk fresh and frozen produce, grains like oats and brown rice, and canned or dried beans. They have lots of organic items at very good prices per pound. Produce items like spinach, kale, and bananas intended for smoothies go straight into the freezer so there's no risk of spoilage and waste.

If you have access to a farmer's market or CSA, you can plan your meals based on seasonal finds within those options, and of course, for the ultimate money saver, you can grow your own vegetables.

Shopping at stores that have bulk bins is also an excellent way to stretch your grocery budget further. Bulk bin items are generally significantly cheaper than buying the same packaged item on the shelf in the same store.

Using online retailers like Amazon, Vitacost, Bob's Red Mill, and others is an excellent way to purchase items inexpensively or to find items that you may not be able to purchase locally.

Generally, I do the remainder of my shopping at a local grocery or big box store, buying organic items if I can afford them and purchasing store-brand items rather than name-brand items for cost savings.

Diet staples in this book such as lentils, beans, and whole grains can be purchased at any grocery store. These items are generally very inexpensive and have a long shelf-life.

Lastly, eating a produce-rich, whole-foods vegan diet is an investment in your health which may save you from having to spend extra money in other areas, such as diet-related prescription drugs, fiber supplements, vitamins, and even illness.

Reducing Food Waste

You might not have thought much about food waste in the past. But consider this food-waste trail: every year in America, farmers throw away 6 billion pounds of food that is oddly sized or shaped or not consistent with grocery store standards. Individual grocery stores also throw out an estimated $2,300 of food every single day to make room for new displays and to get rid of food that is past its sell date or is damaged or spoiled. Then, up to 50 percent of food that makes it into the homes of consumers also gets thrown away.

Because this diet is predominately based on fresh produce, and since fruits and vegetables spoil at a faster rate than other foods, here are some additional tools and ideas to keep your produce fresher longer.

Extend the Life of Fresh Produce

Using the "Eat-on-Repeat" plan helps you to prevent food waste because every meal is planned, shopped for, and organized in advance with leftovers being quickly refrigerated or frozen to prevent spoilage.

At the first sign of wilting, kale, spinach, and fresh herbs can be frozen. Freezing maintains most of the flavor and nutrition of the plant while preventing further spoilage. Use the frozen greens and herbs like fresh in recipes, excepting salads, of course, because frozen produce doesn't thaw to looking fresh, just usable. Bananas starting to brown can also be quickly frozen for later use in smoothies or for vegan ice cream.

Learn how to store your fruits and vegetables properly. Potatoes and onions are best kept in a cool dry place, but should be kept away from each other. Tomatoes are best stored at room temperature so they don't become mealy and lose their flavor.

Reusable BPA-Free Green Bags

These are great for storage, as they lengthen the life of fresh produce by reducing ethylene gas that occurs naturally as fruits and vegetables ripen. Likewise, FoodSaver bags that use vacuum suction to remove the air from packaging can keep foods fresh for longer periods of time. Be sure to wash bags well for reuse, and recycle them when possible.

Another option for keeping food fresh longer is purchasing an activated oxygen device for your refrigerator. Brands like Berry Breeze and O3 Pure Fridge Deodorizer and Food Preserver both have good reviews and work to keep your fridge smelling clean and fresh and reduce ethylene gas that causes food spoilage.

FIVE

Meal Plans and Shopping Lists

THIS CHAPTER IS ALL ABOUT keeping things simple! Using the "Eat-on-Repeat" method I described in the previous chapter simplifies your meal plan and makes shopping easier because you are shopping for multiples of the same things.

However, if the particular meals on the list aren't your thing, or if you prefer more variety throughout the week, feel free to add or swap for your favorite recipes and create your own meal plan based on the model I've provided for you here.

The meals in this book (except for the smoothies, which serve one person) are designed to serve four people. I designed them this way to fit the needs of a family, but you can easily adapt them for singles or couples. So, if you are using this diet plan for one person or for two people, I've included grocery lists for you here as well. These lists cut down the grocery volume by half or more. Meal prep for one meal can be refrigerated or frozen to carry over to additional servings later in the week or month.

Each of the four weeks during the diet has a meal plan with a correlated shopping list. Before you plan the shopping for each week, be sure to check your fridge, freezer, and pantry to see what you have on hand and to prevent doubling up. Often you'll already have many of the items that you need, so these lists will be even shorter.

If you have a small kitchen/fridge/pantry, you can shop for fresh produce and groceries two or three times a week, planning the meals as you go. Leftovers can absolutely be used later in the week or frozen for even later, of course with the exception of salad. However salad can still work as leftovers, if individual components are kept apart and not combined with the dressings. Then they can typically keep fresh for a day or two.

As for those on very strict budgets, this may not be the right plan for you and your pocketbook. While this plan should be affordable for most, a predominantly produce-based diet can be out of reach for some who are truly scraping by. Someone once asked me if they could do the original Green Smoothie Challenge on a grocery budget of $50 a week for a family of four. I had to say no. If you are in this situation, you can eat well on a Dr. McDougall-style plan, which is mostly carbohydrate-based, but you probably won't be able to afford a predominantly produce-based diet plan like this one.

Advice for families: Bulk cooking is going to be your best friend. Because you'll be following the Eat-on-Repeat plan, make double or triple batches of soup, mains, and so on, to get you through the week with less time spent in the kitchen. If you have a small kitchen with limited space for storing fresh food, you may want to divide the list and shop two or three times during the week.

Advice for couples: You will be making full recipes without dividing them, which will give you leftovers to use later in the week or that can be frozen for even later use. Sometimes you might find it helpful to make a half batch of food in order to prevent waste, especially for items that may not stay fresh for as long. Menu items that are eaten 3 times in one week are counted in the shopping list as based on a half recipe for the third time you consume that meal. This way, you don't end up with too many odd leftovers. A smart strategy, especially for items that keep well for eating three times during the week, would be to make one and one-half batches to save kitchen prep/cooking time later in the week.

Advice for singles: In order to keep your shopping list appropriately smaller and your fridge from getting overwhelmed, I'm advising you to halve the recipes in this book (excepting smoothies, of course). The meal plan and the shopping list for individuals will reflect this strategy. Halving the recipes will still give you enough food for leftovers for later in the week or to freeze for even later use, but then your fridge and freezer won't be overrun with so many leftovers that you can't possibly eat them all. For the salad recipes in this book, you may not be purchasing individual lettuces listed in the recipe for each salad. Instead, choose 2 large heads of any kind of lettuce that you enjoy to get you through the week. This change will be reflected in your shopping list. Some items, like a head of cabbage or broccoli, can't easily be halved at the grocery store, so be selective and choose smaller items. If you have access to a store which has produce bins that allow you to select and weigh exactly the amount you need instead of purchasing these items prepackaged, take advantage of those situations, as you will end up with less food waste and less cost overall.

Bulk Produce: For the entire 28 days, keep on hand a good supply of the following produce items that store well and that you can purchase in bulk:

- apples
- bananas
- carrots
- fresh ginger
- garlic
- lemons
- limes
- oranges
- potatoes
- red onions
- yellow onions

Weekly Meal and Shopping Plans

WEEK 1

The following is a list of fresh produce you will need to make all of the recipes for the first week (in addition to some of the bulk produce).

Four People

Smoothies (per person)
1 pound fresh baby spinach
1 bunch fresh kale
1 pound frozen mixed berries
1 pound frozen pineapple

Other Fresh/Frozen Produce
4 bunches scallions
3 bunches broccoli
2 small heads of cauliflower
10 red bell peppers
2 green bell peppers
3 zucchini
1 pound sugar snap peas
3 yellow summer squash
1 small green cabbage
1 head baby bok choy
8 ounces fresh baby spinach
3 heads red leaf lettuce
2 heads romaine lettuce
16 ounces baby greens
6 cucumbers
14 Roma tomatoes
1 head kale
1 pound green beans (fresh or frozen)
16 ounces button mushrooms
1 head celery
16 ounces frozen corn
16 ounces frozen spinach

Fresh Herbs
basil
parsley
cilantro
mint

Two People

Smoothies (per person)
1 pound fresh baby spinach
1 bunch fresh kale
1 pound frozen mixed berries
1 pound frozen pineapple

Other Fresh/Frozen Produce
2 bunches scallions
2 bunches broccoli
1 small head of cauliflower
5 red bell peppers
1 green bell pepper
2 zucchini
12 ounces sugar snap peas
2 yellow summer squash
1 small green cabbage
1 head baby bok choy
8 ounces fresh baby spinach
2 heads red leaf lettuce
1 head romaine lettuce
8 ounces baby greens
3 cucumbers
7 Roma tomatoes
1 head kale
12 ounces green beans (fresh or frozen)
8 ounces button mushrooms
1 head celery
8 ounces frozen corn
8 ounces frozen spinach

Fresh Herbs
basil
parsley
cilantro
mint

One Person

Smoothies (one person)
1 pound fresh baby spinach
1 bunch fresh kale
1 pound frozen mixed berries
1 pound frozen pineapple

Other Fresh/Frozen Produce
1 bunch of scallions
1 bunch of broccoli
1 small head of cauliflower
2 red bell peppers
1 green bell pepper
1 zucchini
4 ounces sugar snap peas
1 yellow summer squash
1 small green cabbage
1 head baby bok choy
4 ounces fresh baby spinach
2 large heads lettuce (any kind)
2 cucumbers
3 Roma tomatoes
1 small head kale
4 ounces green beans (fresh or frozen)
4 ounces button mushrooms
1 small head celery
4 ounces frozen corn
8 ounces frozen spinach

Fresh Herbs
basil
parsley
cilantro
mint

Week 2

The following is a list of fresh produce you will need to make all of the recipes for the second week (in addition to some of the bulk produce).

Four People

Smoothies (per person)
1 pound fresh baby spinach
1 bunch fresh kale
2 pounds frozen blueberries
1 pound frozen peaches

Other Fresh/Frozen Produce
2 bunches scallions
4 small jalapeños
4 small bunches broccoli
1 small head cauliflower
6 red bell peppers
2 green bell peppers
3 large Hass avocados
12 medium zucchinis
1 small purple cabbage
8 ounces fresh baby spinach
3 heads green leaf lettuce
2 heads romaine lettuce
6 cucumbers
20 Roma tomatoes
3 large heads kale
2 pounds frozen corn
8 ounces button mushrooms
1 head celery
1 pound frozen strawberries
1 pound frozen cherries

Fresh Herbs
basil
parsley
cilantro
mint

Two People

Smoothies (per person)
1 pound fresh baby spinach
1 bunch fresh kale
2 pounds frozen blueberries
1 pound frozen peaches

Other Fresh/Frozen Produce
1 bunch scallions
2 small jalapeños
2 small bunches broccoli
1 small head cauliflower
3 red bell peppers
1 green bell pepper
2 large Hass avocados
8 medium zucchinis
1 small purple cabbage
8 ounces fresh baby spinach
2 heads green leaf lettuce
1 head romaine lettuce
3 cucumbers
15 Roma tomatoes
2 large heads kale
1 1/2 pounds frozen corn
4 ounces button mushrooms
1 head celery
1 pound frozen strawberries
1 pound frozen cherries

Fresh Herbs
basil
parsley
cilantro
mint

One Person

Smoothies (one person)
1 pound fresh baby spinach
1 bunch fresh kale
2 pounds frozen blueberries
1 pound frozen peaches

Other Fresh/Frozen Produce
1 bunch scallions
1 small jalapeño
1 small bunch of broccoli
1 small head of cauliflower
2 red bell peppers
1 green bell pepper
1 large Hass avocados
4 medium zucchinis
1 small purple cabbage
2 large heads of lettuce: pick one
   or two varieties
2 cucumbers
8 Roma tomatoes
1 large head of kale
1 pound frozen corn
4 ounces button mushrooms
1 head celery
small package of frozen
   strawberries
small package of frozen cherries

Fresh Herbs
basil
parsley
cilantro
mint

Week 3

The following is a list of fresh produce you will need to make all of the recipes for the third week (in addition to some of the bulk produce).

Four People

Smoothies (per person)
1 avocado
1 bunch fresh kale
1 bunch fresh mint
1 cucumber
1 pound fresh baby spinach

Other Fresh/Frozen Produce
3 small heads green cabbage
1 small head purple cabbage
2 large heads romaine lettuce
4 avocados
1 pound frozen corn
2 bunches fresh radishes
9 Anaheim peppers
3 red bell peppers
9 Roma tomatoes
16 ounces frozen spinach
4 medium cucumbers
4 small heads cauliflower
2 heads green leaf lettuce
16 ounces of fresh button
  mushrooms
1 pound frozen baby peas
8 ounces baby spinach
8 ounces fresh or frozen
  blueberries
3 medium-sized peaches

Fresh Herbs
basil
cilantro
dill
mint
parsley

Two People

Smoothies (per person)
1 avocado
1 bunch fresh kale
1 bunch fresh mint
1 cucumber
1 pound fresh baby spinach

Other Fresh/Frozen Produce
2 small heads green cabbage
1 small head purple cabbage
2 large heads romaine lettuce
2 avocados
8 ounces frozen corn
1 bunch fresh radishes
5 Anaheim peppers
2 red bell peppers
5 Roma tomatoes
16 ounces frozen spinach
2 medium cucumbers
2 small heads of cauliflower
1 head of green leaf lettuce
12 ounces of fresh button
  mushrooms
1 pound frozen baby peas
8 ounces baby spinach
8 ounces fresh or frozen
  blueberries
3 medium-sized peaches

Fresh Herbs
basil
cilantro
dill
mint
parsley

One Person

Smoothies (per person)
1 avocado
1 bunch fresh kale
1 bunch fresh mint
1 cucumber
1 pound fresh baby spinach

Other Fresh/Frozen Produce
1 small head green cabbage
1 small head purple cabbage
2 large heads of preferred
  lettuce
1 avocado
small package of frozen corn
1 bunch fresh radishes
3 Anaheim peppers
1 red bell pepper
3 Roma tomatoes
10 ounces frozen spinach
1 medium cucumber
1 small heads of cauliflower
8 ounces of fresh button
  mushrooms
small package frozen baby peas
4 ounces baby spinach
small package fresh or frozen
  blueberries
1 large peach

Fresh Herbs
basil
cilantro
dill
mint
parsley

Week 4

The following is a list of fresh produce you will need to make all of the recipes for the fourth week (in addition to some of the bulk produce).

Four People

Smoothies (per person)
16 ounces frozen cherries
16 ounces frozen mango
1 pound fresh baby spinach
1 bunch kale

Other Fresh/Frozen Produce
2 pounds fresh spinach
18 Roma tomatoes
3 avocados
2 heads celery
2 bunches scallions
4 heads butter or bib lettuce
2 pounds baby red or Yukon Gold potatoes
2 pounds slender green beans
2 large butternut squash
8 red bell peppers
2 large sweet potatoes
5 heads kale
4 small eggplants
8 medium zucchinis
2 green bell peppers
16 ounces frozen corn
16 ounces fresh or frozen berries

Fresh Herbs
cilantro
parsley
chives
rosemary
tarragon

Two People

Smoothies (per person)
16 ounces frozen cherries
16 ounces frozen mango
1 pound fresh baby spinach
1 bunch kale

Other Fresh/Frozen Produce
1 pound fresh spinach
9 Roma tomatoes
2 avocados
1 head celery
1 bunch scallions
1 head butter or bib lettuce
1 pound baby red or Yukon Gold potatoes
1 1/2 pounds slender green beans
1 large butternut squash
4 red bell peppers
1 large sweet potatoes
3 heads kale
2 small eggplants
4 medium zucchinis
1 green bell peppers
8 ounces frozen corn
8 ounces fresh or frozen berries

Fresh Herbs
cilantro
parsley
chives
rosemary
tarragon

One Person

Smoothies (one person)
16 ounces frozen cherries
16 ounces frozen mango
1 pound fresh baby spinach
1 bunch kale

Other Fresh/Frozen Produce
8 ounces fresh spinach
5 Roma tomatoes
1 avocado
1 head celery
1 bunch scallions
1 head butter or bib lettuce
8 ounces pounds baby red or Yukon Gold potatoes
1 pound slender green beans
1 small butternut squash
2 red bell peppers
1 small sweet potato
2 heads kale
1 small eggplant
2 medium zucchinis
1 green bell pepper
small package of frozen corn
4 ounces fresh or frozen berries

Fresh Herbs
cilantro
parsley
chives
rosemary
tarragon

General Pantry Checklist

The following list includes the pantry ingredients (both perishable and non-perishable) needed if you were to make the all of the recipes in this book. Don't panic: you don't need to buy all these items at once! In fact, you probably already have many of these ingredients on hand in your pantry, freezer, and refrigerator, so use this list more as a checklist in case you need to fill in with a few ingredients.

Refrigerated items
bottled lemon juice
bottled lime juice
dill pickle relish
extra-firm tofu (14-ounce package)
kalamata olives
medjool dates
mellow white miso
sambal olek chili paste
sriracha or other hot sauce
unsweetened plain almond milk
unsweetened plain coconut milk (carton)
unsweetened plain soy milk
vegan probiotic powder

Frozen items
blueberries
corn kernels
mangos
mixed berries
mixed tropical fruit
peaches
pineapple
spinach

Canned Goods
artichoke hearts, in brine
light coconut milk
black beans
cannellini beans
chickpeas/garbanzo beans
great northern beans
kidney beans
navy beans
diced tomatoes

petite diced tomatoes
tomato paste

Nuts and Seeds/ Nut and Seed Butters
almond butter
chia seeds
coconut butter (made from whole coconut, not the non-dairy butter like spread)
flax seeds
hemp seeds
natural peanut butter
PB2 or defatted peanut flour
poppy seeds
raw almonds (bulk)
raw cashew pieces (bulk)
raw pecans (bulk)
raw walnuts (bulk)
roasted peanuts
sesame seeds
slivered almonds
tahini

Plant-Based Sweeteners
agave
date sugar (made from dried dates)
liquid stevia
powdered stevia
pure maple syrup

Gluten-Free Flours and Starches
chickpea flour/garbanzo flour/ besan/gram
gluten-free oat flour
masa harina (finely ground corn flour)

non-GMO cornstarch or arrow-root flour
sorghum flour
superfine ground almond flour
tapioca flour/starch (same thing)

Spices and Seasonings
Bragg's Liquid Aminos, coconut aminos, or tamari
cayenne
chai spice
chili powder
chipotle powder
coriander pods
crushed red pepper flakes
cumin seeds
curry powder
dried basil
dried chives
dried dill
dried ginger
dried onion flakes
dried oregano
dried thyme
fennel seeds
garlic powder
ground black pepper
ground cardamom
ground cinnamon
ground cloves
ground coriander
ground cumin
ground nutmeg
Italian seasonings
kala namak (black salt)
liquid smoke
Mrs. Dash or other no-salt seasoning blend

mustard powder
nutritional yeast
onion flakes
onion powder
red curry paste
red curry powder
sea salt
sesame oil, toasted
smoked paprika
turmeric

Grains and Dried Legumes
French green lentils
gluten-free instant oats
gluten-free rolled oats
gluten-free steel cut oats
green or brown lentils
green or yellow split peas
long grain brown rice
quinoa
split red lentils

Baking Goods
baking powder
baking soda
dairy-free dark chocolate chips
dried unsweetened coconut
    (shreds or flakes)
unsweetened cocoa powder
vanilla

Vinegars and Cooking Wines
apple cider vinegar
balsamic vinegar
dry sherry
mirin
red wine vinegar
rice vinegar
white wine vinegar

Other
All-fruit raspberry jam
apple butter

bean thread noodles
bottled marinara sauce
brown rice pasta shapes
capers
dried apricots
dried cranberries
dried currants
dry-pack sundried tomatoes
golden raisins
raisins
rice paper wrappers for spring
    rolls
shelf-stable silken tofu
tamarind paste
unsweetened applesauce in
    4-ounce containers
vegetable broth paste, cubes, or
    broth

Part 3
The Recipes

Recipe List

Six

Green Smoothies

GREEN SMOOTHIES ARE ONE OF THE BEST breakfast options. They are the basis of the original Green Smoothie Challenge on my website and the perfect solution to hurried mornings when you want your breakfast to pack a strong punch of nutrition but you don't have time to cook, or you need to take your meal on the go.

Drinking green smoothies can fill your need for greens on those days when you don't feel like having a big salad. They also make a good interim meal between breakfast and a later lunch.

All of my green smoothie recipes in this chapter make about one quart, which equals four cups. I serve the smoothies in quart mason jars, and I like to sip them using a glass or stainless steel straw. If you plan to take your smoothies on the go, you will want to invest in a couple of sipper lids created especially for mason jars to prevent spills. I like the Cuppow brand.

Because these smoothies are big, they are very filling. You may find it difficult at first to drink a whole smoothie! If that is the case for you, you can certainly halve a recipe or prepare the smoothie as-is and share it with someone in your household. Additionally, smoothies keep well in the refrigerator for about 10 to 12 hours, so you can have some for breakfast and drink the rest later in the day as hunger strikes. Smoothies can also be frozen and left to defrost overnight in the refrigerator for a cold treat in the summertime.

Luckily, even though these smoothies are huge, they are also a nutrient-dense and low-calorie option. A high-speed blender like a Blendtec works best for creating uniformly smooth drinks without any chunks of fruit or ice. However, a regular blender will work just fine, though you may just need to blend a little longer and or wait for your fruit to slightly defrost in order to really get things moving in your blender.

I've included the addition of a tablespoon of flax, hemp, or chia seeds in each smoothie. These superfood ingredients will make your smoothies thicker, creamier, and more filling. They also pack a hefty punch of omega-3 fats. Experiment and find out which ingredient is your favorite. If you are getting enough omega-3s and other healthy fats through other recipes, feel free to leave the seeds out.

If you want to simplify smoothie time, you can tightly pack all of the fruits and vegetables you need for a recipe into a quart-sized Ziploc bag, making sure to leave out any required liquid or ice. Simply remove a bag from the freezer and add the contents to your blender.

In this case, I recommend omitting the ice and replacing it with liquid as needed to blend. If you don't have a high-speed blender and you want to use this time-saving trick, consider adding lukewarm water or liquid to your smoothie to help the fruit and vegetables defrost and blend quickly.

If you prefer creamier smoothies, you can substitute unsweetened plant milk for some or all of the water in recipes without plant milk. Be sure to use unsweetened plant milk to avoid unnecessary sugar and calories.

To sweeten my smoothies, I love to use liquid stevia. The amount needed will depend on your personal tastes and also on the natural tartness of the ingredients in each smoothie. Some of my testers for this cookbook used no added stevia, some of them used just a few drops of stevia. I like my smoothies on the sweeter side, so you will have to experiment and find out what works best for you. I typically add one dropper of liquid stevia if making a smoothie for myself. If I'm making a smoothie for my children, I use 1 1/2 to 2 droppers.

Smoothies are frosty and refreshing in the summer, but in cold weather they can be less appealing. To solve this problem, create smoothies that are less cold by using all fresh or defrosted frozen fruit instead of fruit directly from the freezer. You can also omit the ice to take off some of the chill. Some of my testers enjoyed following up their smoothie with a steaming cup of herbal tea.

Lastly, the recipes in this chapter are guidelines for creating delicious smoothies, but many of the recipes can be mixed and matched to create new favorite smoothies. If you are a green smoothie novice, you may find it easier and tastier to use all fresh spinach in your smoothies and slowly introduce kale or other dark leafy greens as you develop a palate for them.

Apple Pie Green Smoothie

This smoothie is surprisingly reminiscent of apple pie. It is really delicious and I think you'll find it one of your fast favorites. The fiber from the apples also keeps your stomach full for a long time, so this is a favorite smoothie of mine to take out and about when I'm running errands all morning and need something to tide me over until I get home.

- 1 cup water
- 2 cups packed organic baby spinach
- 1 medium banana
- 2 small apples, cored and quartered
- 1 tablespoon organic apple butter or 1 date, pitted and snipped into small pieces, or 2 tablespoons Date Paste (page 16)
- 1 teaspoon ground cinnamon
- 1 1/2 cups ice cubes
- 1 tablespoon ground flaxseed, chia seed, or hemp seed (optional)
- Liquid stevia, to taste (optional)

In a blender, combine the water, spinach, banana, apples, apple butter, cinnamon, ice, and flaxseed, if using. Blend the mixture until completely smooth, creamy, and well combined, about 1 to 2 minutes. Add the liquid stevia, if using, and pulse to incorporate.

MAKES 1 SERVING (ABOUT 1 QUART)

Annie's Da Cherry Bomb Smoothie

Annie of An Unrefined Vegan emailed me the recipe to this smoothie the first time we did the Green Smoothie Challenge together. It has been one of my favorites ever since. Frozen cherries are sometimes difficult to find, so if you come upon them, make sure you snatch multiple bags so you can make this smoothie often!

- 1 cup unsweetened almond milk
- 2 cups packed fresh baby spinach
- 1 medium banana
- 1 1/2 cups frozen cherries
- 1/4 teaspoon ground cinnamon
- 1 cup water or 1 1/2 cups ice for a creamier, colder smoothie
- 1 tablespoon ground flaxseed, chia seeds, or hemp seed (optional)
- Liquid stevia, to taste (optional)

In a blender, combine the almond milk, spinach, banana, cherries, cinnamon, water (or ice) and flaxseed, if using. Blend the mixture until completely smooth, creamy, and well combined, 1 to 2 minutes. Add the liquid stevia, if using, and pulse to incorporate.

MAKES 1 SERVING (ABOUT 1 QUART)

Variation: To make this a Mayan Cherry Smoothie, add a tiny dash cayenne pepper and 2 tablespoons unsweetened raw cacao powder or unsweetened cocoa powder.

Blueberry Vanilla Green Smoothie

This smoothie reminds me of a blueberry muffin! It is satisfying, creamy, and sweet. This smoothie is also delicious with cherries instead of blueberries. One of my testers uses a teaspoon of maca in this smoothie to make it even more supercharged!

    1 cup unsweetened almond milk
    1 cup water
    1 cup packed fresh baby spinach
    1 cup packed fresh kale
    1 medium banana
    1 1/2 cups frozen blueberries
    1/4 to 1/2 teaspoon vanilla extract
    1/2 cup ice
    1 tablespoon ground flaxseed, chia seed, or hemp seed (optional)
    Liquid stevia, to taste (optional)

In a blender, combine the almond milk, water, spinach, kale, banana, blueberries, vanilla, ice, and flaxseed, if using. Blend the mixture until completely smooth, creamy, and well combined, 1 to 2 minutes. Add the liquid stevia, if using, and pulse to incorporate.

MAKES 1 SERVING (ABOUT 1 QUART)

Tropical Colada Green Smoothie

Of all the smoothies in this chapter, my testers unanimously loved this one the most!

1 cup unsweetened almond or coconut milk from a carton (not canned)
2 cups packed spinach
1 medium navel orange, peeled and quartered
1 medium banana
1 cup fresh or frozen pineapple
1 tablespoon dried unsweetened coconut shreds
1 1/2 cups ice
Liquid stevia, to taste

In a blender, combine the almond milk, spinach, orange, banana, pineapple, coconut shreds, and ice. Blend the mixture until completely smooth, creamy, and combined, 1 to 2 minutes. Add the liquid stevia to taste and pulse to incorporate.

MAKES 1 SERVING (ABOUT 1 QUART)

Mango Madness Green Smoothie

This smoothie is so creamy and dreamy it's hard to believe it's not a dessert! To make this taste like a mango lassi, add 1/4 cup silken tofu and 1/4 teaspoon cardamom.

1 cup unsweetened almond milk
1 cup water
2 cups packed fresh baby spinach
1 medium banana
1 1/2 cups frozen mango pieces
1/2 cup ice
1 tablespoon ground flaxseed, chia seed, or hemp seed (optional)
Liquid stevia, to taste (optional)

In a blender, combine the almond milk, water, spinach, banana, mango, ice, and flaxseed, if using. Blend the mixture until completely smooth, creamy, and combined, about 1 to two minutes. Add the liquid stevia, if using, and pulse to incorporate.

MAKES 1 SERVING (ABOUT 1 QUART)

Orange Pineapple Pomegranate Bliss

This smoothie is every bit as blissful and delightful as it sounds with the citrus, pineapple and pomegranate creating a wonderful trio of flavors bursting with goodness, antioxidants and vitamin C. It's hard to believe something so good for you can taste this yummy!

1 cup water
2 cups packed fresh baby spinach or kale
1 medium banana
2 tablespoons orange zest, from the orange below
1 medium navel orange, zested, peeled and quartered
1/4 cup frozen pineapple
1/2 cup pomegranate arils or 1/2 cup unsweetened pomegranate juice
1 1/2 cups ice
1 tablespoon ground flaxseed, chia seed, or hemp seed (optional)
Liquid stevia, to taste (optional)

In a blender, combine the water, spinach or kale, banana, orange zest, orange, pineapple, pomegranate, ice and flaxseed, if using. Blend the mixture until completely smooth, creamy and combined, 1 to 2 minutes. Add the liquid stevia, if using, and pulse to incorporate.

MAKES 1 SERVING (ABOUT 1 QUART)

Green Julius

This smoothie reminds me of that too-sweet and frothy orange smoothie that you can get at the mall, but without being overly sweet or frothy or leaving the sick feeling in your tummy afterwards. It is one of my all-time favorites.

1 cup unsweetened almond milk
1 cup packed fresh baby spinach
1 cup packed fresh kale
1 medium banana
Zest of one medium orange
2 medium navel oranges, (1 zested for ingredient above), peeled, and quartered
1 1/2 cups ice
1 tablespoon ground flaxseed, chia seed, or hemp seed (optional)
Liquid stevia, to taste (optional)

In a blender, combine the almond milk, spinach, kale, banana, orange zest, oranges, ice, and flaxseed, if using. Blend the mixture until completely smooth, creamy and well combined, 1 to 2 minutes. Add the liquid stevia, if using, and pulse to incorporate.

MAKES 1 SERVING (ABOUT 1 QUART)

Poppy's Jaffa Cake Smoothie

For those of you not in the know, the term "jaffa" refers to something with orange and chocolate. In my opinion, it is one of the most delightful combinations on earth! I had been thinking of a chocolate orange smoothie, but one of my testers, Poppy, beat me to it. She's given permission for the recipe to be used here. You can find Poppy at her famed blog, Bunny Kitchen.

- 1 cup unsweetened almond milk
- 2 cups fresh packed baby spinach or kale
- 1 medium banana
- 2 peeled oranges, plus the zest of 1 orange before peeling
- 2 tablespoons unsweetened cacao powder or unsweetened cocoa powder
- 1 teaspoon vanilla extract
- 1 1/2 cups ice cubes
- 1 tablespoon ground flax, chia seed, or hemp seed (optional)
- Liquid stevia (optional)

In a blender, combine the almond milk, spinach, banana, orange, orange zest, cacao powder, vanilla, ice, and flaxseed, if using. Blend the mixture until completely smooth, creamy, and combined, 1 to 2 minutes. Add the liquid stevia to taste, if using, and pulse to incorporate.

MAKES 1 SERVING (ABOUT 1 QUART)

Razzleberry Lemonade Green Smoothie

This smoothie is tart, delicious, cooling, and refreshing. If you don't like kale in your smoothie, feel free to replace it with fresh baby spinach. (See photo, opposite.)

- **1 1/2 cups water**
- **2 cups packed kale**
- **1 medium banana**
- **1 1/2 cups frozen mixed berries**
- **1/4 small lemon, with or without peel (if organic lemons, you can leave the peel on)**
- **1/2 cup ice**
- **1 tablespoon ground flaxseed, chia seed, or hemp seed (optional)**
- **Liquid stevia, to taste**

In the blender, combine the water, kale, banana, mixed berries, lemon, ice, and flaxseed, if using. Blend the mixture until completely smooth, creamy, and combined, 1 to 2 minutes. Add the liquid stevia, to taste, and pulse to incorporate.

MAKES 1 SERVING (ABOUT 1 QUART)

Spotted Peach Green Smoothie

This smoothie uses chia seeds, but don't blend them! Leave them whole for a "spotty" smoothie!

- **2 cups water**
- **1 cup packed fresh baby spinach**
- **1 cup packed fresh kale**
- **1 medium banana**
- **1 1/2 cups frozen peaches**
- **1/2 cup ice**
- **Liquid stevia, to taste**
- **1 tablespoon chia seeds, stirred in after blending**

In a blender, combine the water, spinach, kale, banana, peaches, and ice. Blend the mixture until completely smooth and creamy, 1 to 2 minutes. Add the stevia to taste and pulse to incorporate. Stir in the chia seeds and enjoy your spotted smoothie!

MAKES 1 SERVING (ABOUT 1 QUART)

Razzleberry Lemonade Green Smoothie (opposite, top)

Chocolate-Covered Blues Green Smoothie

I made this smoothie one day when I was really craving chocolate but wanted a healthy option instead of a chocolate bar. I was surprised by how much I loved the combination and how well it satisfied my chocolate cravings.

- 1 cup unsweetened almond milk
- 1 cup water
- 2 cups packed fresh baby spinach or fresh kale
- 1 medium banana
- 1 1/2 cups frozen blueberries
- 2 tablespoons unsweetened raw cacao powder (or regular unsweetened cocoa powder)
- 1/4 teaspoon vanilla extract
- 1/2 cup ice
- 1 tablespoon ground flaxseed, chia seed, or hemp seed (optional)
- Liquid stevia, to taste (optional)

In a blender, combine the almond milk, water, spinach, banana, blueberries, cacao powder, vanilla, ice, and flaxseed, if using. Blend the mixture until completely smooth, creamy, and combined, 1 to 2 minutes. Add the liquid stevia, if using, and pulse to incorporate.

MAKES 1 SERVING (ABOUT 1 QUART)

Ultra-Alkalizing Green Smoothie

This smoothie is a very powerful, all green vegetable alkalizing smoothie without any fruit (excepting lime). It is not a smoothie for the faint of heart, but I promise it grows on you and makes you feel fantastic. If you wake up in the morning with a foggy brain, or if you suffer from recurrent candida, this smoothie is for you! Because of the nature of this smoothie, you may need to blend it longer if you don't have a powerful blender to get it fully blended without any chunks.

1 cup water
1 (6-inch) cucumber, cut into 1-inch slices
2 celery ribs, cut into 1-inch slices (can include leafy green tops)
1 1-inch piece fresh ginger, scrubbed but not peeled
2 cups packed baby spinach
1 small lime, peeled and quartered
1/4 cup roughly chopped parsley
2 tablespoons almond butter
1 cup ice
Liquid stevia, to taste (I use two droppers in this recipe)

In a blender, combine the water, cucumber, celery, ginger, spinach, lime, parsley, and almond butter. Blend the mixture until completely smooth, creamy, and combined, 2 minutes. Add the ice and liquid stevia and blend until smooth.

MAKES 1 SERVING (ABOUT 1 QUART)

Variation: For a sweeter smoothie, add one small tart green apple.

Carrot Cake Waffles (page 70)

SEVEN

Breakfast

SOME PEOPLE ENVISION BREAKFAST as big plates of pancakes, waffles, omelets or scrambles, and hash browns served with a side of bacon or sausage. All of the above options are typically heavy, calorie-laden foods full of sugars, refined carbohydrates, and animal products. Other people may simply consider breakfast a cup of coffee on the go, a slice or two of toast, or a quick bowl of cold cereal. However, none of these are the most nutritious or well-rounded options.

You've probably heard since childhood that breakfast is the most important meal of the day. This is true for a lot of reasons. If you start your day with a healthy meal, you are more likely to continue with healthy eating habits throughout the day. Plant-based breakfasts that are nutritious and filling will keep you sustained and give you energy to accomplish the things you need to do. Eating a healthy and hearty breakfast also prevents overeating or bingeing later in the day as hunger strikes.

With these points in mind, I've designed the recipes in this chapter to mimic some of these classic comfort food breakfast favorites and provide you with healthier options to include in your routine. Many of my recipe testers prepared these breakfast meals on weekends and drank the green smoothies for breakfasts during weekdays, but you can have one of these great breakfast options in the morning and have a smoothie later in the day as a mid-afternoon meal. You can even have a non-traditional breakfast for dinner. You can also eat one of these meals for a mid-morning second breakfast without sabotaging your diet plan.

Apple and Chai Spice Muesli

For convenience, this muesli can be soaked overnight so it's ready when you are in the morning. If you aren't a fan of chai spice, you can substitute 2 teaspoons of ground cinnamon for the chai spice mix for an Apple Cinnamon Muesli. Raw chopped pecans or walnuts can also be used in place of the almonds or hazelnuts.

2 cups rolled oats (gluten-free if needed)
2 teaspoons ground chai spice
1/4 cup roughly chopped raw almonds or raw hazelnuts
4 large cored unpeeled apples, shredded
2 cups unsweetened almond milk
1 tablespoon lemon juice
1/4 cup Date Paste (page 16)
A pinch of fine sea salt

In a large bowl, combine the rolled oats, chai spice, almonds or hazelnuts, and apples. Add the almond milk, lemon juice, date paste and sea salt. Stir to combine all of the ingredients. This can be left to soak for 20 to 30 minutes and then eaten, or it can be refrigerated overnight.

MAKES 4 SERVINGS

Note: If you can't easily find chai spice, you should be able to find an herbal chai tea at your local grocery store. Simply boil the almond milk, steep 2 to 4 tea bags in the almond milk for 5 to 10 minutes, then proceed with the recipe.

Carrot Cake Waffles

Some mornings, we all wish we could have a slice of cake for breakfast and not have it affect our waistlines. This recipe is for those mornings. It feels super indulgent and naughty while being delicious and super good for you at the same time. (See photo on page 66.)

1 1/3 cups Somer's All-Purpose Gluten-Free Flour Blend (page 14)

2 tablespoons ground golden flaxseed

1/4 teaspoon stevia powder

1 tablespoon baking powder

1 teaspoon ground cinnamon

1/2 teaspoon ground ginger

1/4 teaspoon ground nutmeg

1/4 teaspoon ground cloves

1/4 teaspoon sea salt

1 cup finely shredded carrots (2 medium-sized carrots)

2 tablespoons roughly chopped walnuts or pecans

1/4 cup raisins (optional)

1 teaspoon orange zest

1 cup unsweetened almond milk

1 teaspoon vanilla extract

1/2 teaspoon apple cider vinegar

Preheat the waffle maker. In a medium-sized bowl, combine the flour, ground flaxseed, stevia powder, baking powder, cinnamon, ginger, nutmeg, cloves, and salt. Whisk until fully combined. Add the carrots, walnuts, raisins (if using), and orange zest. Stir to combine.

In a small bowl, whisk together the almond milk, vanilla, and vinegar. This will create a vegan buttermilk. Add the wet ingredients to the flour mixture and stir until the batter is just combined.

Let the batter rest for 10 minutes while the flaxseed thickens the batter and the batter rises; it may nearly double. Spray the waffle iron with a quick mist of pan spray. Scoop one quarter of the batter, about an overflowing 1/2 cup, onto your waffle iron. Let the waffles bake for 6 to 8 minutes or until golden and crispy on the outside. Resist the temptation to check on them until they have cooked for 6 minutes, otherwise they may fall apart. Repeat the same procedure with the remaining waffles. Let the waffles cool for about 5 minutes. If you eat them before this point, they may have slightly gummy centers.

MAKES 4 SERVINGS

Variation: If desired, you can top each waffle with a drizzle of creamy caramel sauce. Mix 1/4 cup Date Paste (page 16) with 1/4 cup Cashew Cream (page 15) until well combined. Each waffle gets two tablespoons of topping.

Note: Waffle irons can vary greatly in temperature and size. To learn about yours, bake the waffles for 6 minutes without opening the waffle iron to check on them. Then, if they need additional baking time, close the waffle iron and bake for a minute or two longer. My waffle iron is 6 inches in diameter. If yours is bigger, simply measure out the specified amount—about one heaping half cup—and pour in the center of your waffle iron. It won't spread all the way to the edge of the waffle iron, but you will get the appropriate-sized breakfast. For a smaller waffle iron, use less batter and bake according to the directions above, reducing cooking time by a minute or two if necessary.

Florentine Tofu Scramble

My tester Tami, from the blog Nutmeg Notebook, made a Mexican version of this scramble by using fire-roasted tomatoes with green chilies. You could use a can of Ro-Tel tomatoes and replace the basil in this ingredient list with cilantro. Try topping that version with some Fire-Roasted Salsa (page 155) and Cashew Sour Cream (page 154).

- 1 (14-ounce) package extra-firm tofu, drained, patted dry, and crumbled
- 1 (14.5-ounce) can fire-roasted diced tomatoes, undrained
- 4 tablespoons nutritional yeast
- 2 scallions, cut into 1/4-inch diagonal slices
- 1 teaspoon fine sea salt (or for an eggy flavor, use kala namak – black salt)
- 1/2 teaspoon ground black pepper
- 1 teaspoon dried oregano
- 4 cups chopped fresh baby spinach
- 1/4 cup packed fresh basil, roughly chopped

In a large nonstick skillet, sauté the tofu and the fire-roasted diced tomatoes over medium-high heat until the liquid from the diced tomatoes is nearly evaporated. Add the nutritional yeast, scallions, salt, pepper, and oregano. Cook for 1 to 2 minutes longer to let the flavors absorb.

Stir in the spinach and cook until it is slightly wilted. Remove the skillet from the heat and sprinkle with the basil before serving.

MAKES 4 SERVINGS

Bananas Foster Pancakes

In this recipe, cooking banana slices directly in the pancake causes the bananas to caramelize beautifully without your having to dirty an extra skillet. However, this recipe requires a true nonstick skillet, otherwise these pancakes may stick like crazy!

- 1 1/3 cups Somer's All-Purpose Gluten-Free Flour Blend (page 14)
- 2 tablespoons ground golden flaxseed
- 1/4 teaspoon stevia powder
- 1 tablespoon baking powder
- 1/2 teaspoon ground cinnamon
- 1/4 teaspoon sea salt
- 1 1/4 cups unsweetened almond milk
- 1 teaspoon vanilla extract
- 1/2 teaspoon apple cider vinegar
- 2 ripe medium bananas, cut into 1/2-inch slices, divided
- Date Paste (page 16), optional

In a medium-sized bowl, combine the flour, flaxseed, stevia, baking powder, cinnamon, and salt. Whisk until the dry ingredients are fully combined.

In a small bowl, whisk together the almond milk, vanilla, and vinegar. This will create a vegan buttermilk.

Add the wet ingredients to the flour mixture and stir until the batter is just combined.

Let the batter rest for 10 minutes while the flaxseed thickens the batter and the batter rises; it may nearly double. In the meantime, heat a large nonstick skillet over medium heat and mist with a tiny bit of nonstick spray if desired.

Pour the batter into 4-inch rounds. Cook the pancakes for 30 seconds and then press some of the banana slices into each pancake. Cook the pancakes for 2 minutes more, or until the bubbles have burst in each of them and the tops start to appear dry. Flip the pancakes and cook for 1 to 2 minutes more. You should get 12 pancakes total. Top pancakes with the remaining sliced banana and a schmear of date paste, if using.

MAKES 4 SERVINGS

Note: If you have a large nonstick griddle or large electric skillet griddle, you can cook multiple pancakes at once.

Quinoa Berry Banana Bowls

If you like a sweeter breakfast, top this cereal with a tablespoon of Date Paste (page 16) or add a few drops of liquid stevia to the almond milk.

- 4 scant cups cooked quinoa
- 2 cups unsweetened almond milk
- 2 cups fresh or frozen mixed berries
- 2 bananas
- 4 teaspoons hemp seeds

In each of four cereal-sized bowls, place 1 scant cup of the cooked quinoa, 1/2 cup of the almond milk, 1/2 cup of the berries, and 1/2 of a sliced banana. Top each bowl with one teaspoon of the hemp seeds.

MAKES 4 SERVINGS

Vegan Chocolate Buttermilk Pancakes

Everybody deserves to have a little (healthy) chocolate for breakfast once in a while. These pancakes got five-star reviews from all of my testers. I think you will agree with their rating. This recipe requires a true nonstick skillet to keep the pancakes from sticking. Serve with whatever fresh fruit you like—we enjoy them with strawberries, raspberries, bananas, or a combination of all three.

> 1 1/4 cups Somer's All-Purpose Gluten-Free Flour Blend (page 14)
> 2 tablespoons unsweetened cocoa powder
> 1 tablespoon baking powder
> 1 tablespoon ground golden flaxseed
> 1 tablespoon vegan mini chocolate chips, optional (I like Lily's stevia-sweetened or Enjoy Life)
> 1/4 teaspoon sea salt
> 1 cup unsweetened almond milk
> 1 tablespoon pure maple syrup or 1/4 teaspoon stevia powder
> 1 teaspoon vanilla extract
> 1 tablespoon apple cider vinegar
> 1/4 cup unsweetened applesauce

In a medium-sized bowl, combine the flour, cocoa powder, baking powder, flax, chocolate chips, and salt. Whisk until the dry ingredients are fully combined. In a small bowl, whisk together the almond milk, maple syrup, vanilla, and vinegar. This will create a vegan buttermilk for your pancakes. Add the vegan buttermilk and the applesauce to the flour mixture and stir until the batter is just combined.

Let the batter rest for 10 minutes while the flaxseed thickens the batter and the batter rises; it may nearly double.

Heat a large nonstick skillet over medium heat and mist with a tiny bit of nonstick spray, if desired. Scoop the batter into 3-inch rounds. Cook for 2 to 3 minutes or until the bubbles have burst in each of the pancakes and the tops start to appear dry. Flip the pancakes and cook for 1 to 2 minutes more. You should get 12 pancakes total.

MAKES 4 SERVINGS

Note: If you have a large nonstick griddle or a large electric skillet griddle, you can cook multiple pancakes at once.

Raw Neapolitan Overnight Oats

This breakfast can make a lovely morning presentation, and it truly tastes like a dessert. Make sure to plan in advance for this meal since you will need to start preparation the night before.

- 1 1/2 cups steel-cut oats (or certified gluten-free steel-cut oats)
- 4 tablespoons chia seeds
- 3 cups unsweetened almond milk (use homemade Almond Milk, page 15, for a truly raw breakfast)
- 4 tablespoons raw unsweetened cacao powder
- 1/4 cup Date Paste (page 16)
- 2 teaspoons vanilla extract or 1 teaspoon vanilla paste
- 4 medium-sized ripe frozen bananas, cut into 1/2 inch pieces
- 6 to 8 frozen strawberries, cut into 1/2-inch slices (1 heaping cup)

The night before you plan on making this, blend the oats in a blender or grind them in a coffee grinder until fine. Transfer half of the ground oats into each of two quart-sized mason jars. Into each jar, add 2 tablespoons chia seeds, 1 1/2 cups almond milk, and 2 tablespoons date paste.

Add the raw cacao powder to one of the jars and the vanilla extract to the other jar. Put lids on the mason jars and shake until the ingredients are well combined. Now you have one jar of chocolate overnight oats and one jar of vanilla overnight oats.

Put the jars of overnight oats in the refrigerator and leave them overnight. The next morning, blend the frozen bananas in your food processor with a splash or two of almond milk. Process until creamy. Remove half of the mixture and set aside in the freezer. Add the frozen strawberries to the banana mixture remaining in the food processor and process the same way. Now you have raw strawberry and banana ice creams.

Layer and alternate the banana and strawberry ice creams with the chocolate and vanilla overnight oats in clean mason jars or fancy clear glass serving cups as in the photograph. Serve immediately.

MAKES 4 SERVINGS

Vegetable Pudla

This recipe is adapted from one created by Kittee Bee Berns, who blogs at Cake Maker to the Stars. Her website has a section on pudla (Indian chickpea crepes) that is worth exploring. When I first discovered pudla on her site, I was endlessly fascinated. It was like something between an omelet and a pancake and I. Could. Not. Stop. Making. Them. The same thing may happen to you. I have tried multiple variations, as I'm sure you will too, but this one is my favorite. You need a true nonstick skillet to make these in order to get them not to stick without using oil.

- 2 cups chickpea flour (besan)
- 1/8 teaspoon turmeric
- 1/2 teaspoon garlic powder
- 1 teaspoon sea salt (you can use black salt instead of sea salt for an eggier flavor, but don't tell Kittee: she thinks it's stinky)
- 1 teaspoon baking powder
- 1 teaspoon dried dill
- 1/4 teaspoon freshly ground black pepper

- 1 teaspoon mustard powder
- 1 tablespoon nutritional yeast
- 1 cup water
- 2 tablespoons tahini
- 1/4 cup lemon juice
- 2 Roma tomatoes, chopped into 1/2-inch dice
- 1 medium onion, finely chopped
- 1/4 cup roughly chopped fresh parsley
- 2 cups roughly chopped fresh baby spinach

In a large bowl, whisk together the chickpea flour, turmeric, garlic powder, salt, baking powder, dill, black pepper, mustard powder, and nutritional yeast.

In a separate bowl, whisk together the water, tahini, and lemon juice until thoroughly combined. Add the water mixture to the chickpea mixture and stir to fully incorporate. Add the tomatoes, onion, parsley, and spinach and fold into the batter. It will be quite thick! Do not taste the batter as uncooked chickpea batter is not yummy.

Heat a large nonstick skillet over medium heat and, if desired, mist very lightly oil with a spray oil. For best results, cook only one pudla at a time (unless you have a big nonstick griddle or big nonstick electric skillet). Scoop one quarter of the mixture, about one scant cup, onto the skillet and smooth into an 8-inch round with the back of a spoon. Cook the pudla for 4 minutes, or until the bottom has formed a nice golden brown crust and the edges of the pudla are dry, then flip the pudla very carefully with a thin metal spatula. Cook the pudla for an additional 3 to 4 minutes on the other side.

MAKES 4 SERVINGS

Veggie Patch Sunday Morning Omelets

This recipe goes much faster if you make the Fresh Vegan Moxarella (page 16) in advance. It is also helpful to have two people cooking—one making the omelets, the other preparing the fillings—but you certainly can make this on your own. This recipe require a true nonstick skillet. I like the ceramic, environmentally friendly ones. I tried this recipe using my well-seasoned cast iron skillet, and the omelets were much more difficult to flip and turn.

OMELETS

1 1/3 cups chickpea flour

2 tablespoons ground golden flaxseed

3 tablespoons non-GMO cornstarch

2 tablespoons nutritional yeast

1 teaspoon onion powder

1/2 teaspoon garlic powder

1 teaspoon kala namak (black salt) or sea salt

1/4 teaspoon smoked paprika

1/4 teaspoon ground yellow mustard

1/4 teaspoon turmeric

1 teaspoon baking powder

Dash of cayenne pepper

2 cups water

FILLING

1/4 cup vegetable broth

1 medium red onion, thinly sliced

1 small clove minced garlic

1 medium zucchini, cut into 1/2-inch dice

4 cups packed fresh baby spinach

8 ounces button mushrooms, cleaned and dried, cut into 1/4-inch slices

2 Roma tomatoes, cut into 1/2-inch dice

1/4 teaspoon liquid smoke

Salt and ground black pepper

1/2 recipe Fresh Vegan Moxarella (page 16)

Omelets: In a large bowl, combine the chickpea flour, flaxseed, cornstarch, nutritional yeast, onion powder, garlic powder, black salt, smoked paprika, mustard powder, turmeric, baking powder, and cayenne with a wire whisk. Add the water and whisk thoroughly to combine. Do not taste the batter: chickpea flour is not yummy raw.

Let the batter rest for about ten minutes to thicken and absorb the flavors from the spices. Very lightly oil a medium nonstick skillet with oil spray and heat over medium heat.

Scoop about a 3/4 scant cup of your omelet mixture into a skillet and smooth into a 7- to 8-inch round with the back of a spoon. Place a lid over your skillet (if it doesn't come with one, use a lid from a different pan that even sort of fits your skillet). Let the omelet cook undisturbed for 3 to 4 minutes. The steam helps cook the omelet. Remove the lid and check the omelet. If the surface seems dryish, carefully flip it over with a thin spatula. If the surface still feels wet, let it cook for a minute more. Cook on the reverse side for 1 to 2 minutes.

Remove it from heat, place it on a plate, and cover it with a kitchen towel to keep it from drying out. Repeat with the remaining 3 portions of batter.

Filling: Heat the broth in a large skillet over high heat. Add the onion and sauté until nearly translucent, about 5 minutes. Add more broth as necessary to keep the onions from burning. Add the mushrooms and the garlic and cook until the mushrooms start to release their liquid, 3 to 4 minutes more. Add in the spinach 1 cup at a time and let wilt down until all the spinach is added. Add the tomatoes, drizzle with the liquid smoke, and cook for a minute or two more. Season with salt and pepper, to taste.

Assembly: Take one of the omelets and spread a quarter of the Moxarella onto one side. Then add a quarter of the cooked vegetables to the other side. Fold the half of the omelet with the Moxarella over the vegetable half so the cheese is on top of the vegetables. Repeat for each omelet.

MAKES 4 SERVINGS

Optional Additional Toppings: Try a spoonful of Fire-Roasted Salsa (page 155), dollops of Cashew Sour Cream (page 154), a drizzle of Roasted Red Pepper Dressing (page 88), roughly chopped parsley or cilantro, or a light sprinkling of nutritional yeast.

Roasted Red Pepper Dressing (page 88)

Eight

Salads and Dressings

I ADORE A SALAD in which crunchy, fresh, and crispy vegetables all come together in a tasty symphony. When the salad is then loaded with good sources of vegan protein and covered with a delicious salad dressing, the combination is simply heaven. Sometimes there's nothing that I would rather eat.

The salads and dressings in this chapter are the exactly the type you need to keep you from going on a salad hiatus. Although I have paired each salad with the dressing that I think suits it best, all of the salad dressings here are interchangeable, meaning that if you prefer a certain dressing, you can use it on any of the salads you like.

While I do think salads are an important part of dieting, I don't believe they have to look or taste like rabbit food. Eating a big, nutritious, and tasty salad every day fulfills nearly all of your daily requirements for vegetables, and because salads are so nutrient-dense and low in calories, they can fill you up and help you to lose weight. Even if you haven't enjoyed salads previously, I challenge you to make eating salad a habit. In no time you'll find yourself craving all the leafy greens and fresh crisp vegetables that you can get your hands on. For good measure, I've included lots of creative toppings and even a lentil salad and a grain salad for those days where chomping on lettuce doesn't suit your fancy.

The first section of this chapter includes basic salad dressings to dress up any salad you'd like. All of my salad dressings are oil-free and low-fat compared to traditional salad dressings, but they're full of flavor. The best part is that you won't find any hidden chemicals or preservatives in these dressings. I like having two or three dressings in the refrigerator at all times so that salad-making is simplified and an easy choice. Most of the dressings will keep for a minimum of four days, and some will keep for a week to ten days without spoiling. Each salad dressing recipe makes four servings.

You don't need to limit yourself to the two-tablespoon recommended serving size on the back of bottled dressings. You can use 1/4 to 1/3 cup of my dressings per serving—and you'll want that much because many of these dressings are good enough to drink. Don't be daunted by the longer ingredient lists for some of the dressings. I promise they are all super easy to make. The various ingredients make the salad dressings sing with flavor instead of fat.

The big salad recipes in this chapter are intended to be used for a main course meal sometime during your day, either for lunch or dinner, or even as a hefty mid-afternoon meal on a day you plan to have a lighter dinner. You'll also find a few lighter salads that you can use as a side dish to one of the hearty main course meals. They can also be used for a smaller main course meal or as a light and refreshing meal any time during the day if the feeling strikes.

The salads in this chapter serve four people. If you want them to serve one or two people, simply halve or quarter the recipe. Alternatively, you could make the full salad recipe and not combine the ingredients, refrigerating each component separately. If the salads aren't tossed with dressing, the individual ingredients should keep fresh for two to three days, allowing you to have salad leftovers without any additional effort. Salad dressings can also be frozen in individual portions if you think you won't use a complete recipe before it spoils.

Creamy Raspberry Poppy Seed Dressing

Poppy seed dressings are generally heavy, oily, and full of sugar. This one is a lighter take on the traditional formula, using an all-fruit preserve for sweetness, cashews for creaminess, and just the right blend of seasonings and spices for the perfect flavor. You'll love the pretty pink color of this dressing that makes it stand out.

1/3 cup store-bought orange juice or the juice from 1 freshly squeezed navel orange
1/3 cup all-fruit seedless red or black raspberry preserves (no sugar added)
3 tablespoons red wine vinegar
1/4 cup chopped red onion
2 tablespoons raw cashew pieces
1/2 teaspoon ground mustard powder
1/4 teaspoon sea salt, or to taste
1/8 teaspoon ground black pepper
1 tablespoon poppy seeds

In a blender, combine the orange juice, raspberry preserves, vinegar, onion, cashews, mustard powder, salt, and pepper. Blend until smooth and creamy, about 1 minute. Add the poppy seeds to the blender and pulse just until the seeds are evenly distributed.

MAKES ABOUT 1 CUP

Roasted Red Pepper Dressing

This roasted red pepper dressing has a "cheesy" yummy flavor. It makes eating any salad feel like an indulgence. (See photo on page 84.)

- 1 large red bell pepper
- 2 tablespoons raw cashews pieces or 1 tablespoon tahini
- 1 tablespoon lemon or lime juice
- 2 to 4 tablespoons water or more, as needed
- 2 tablespoons mellow white miso
- 1 pitted, chopped soft medjool date (optional)
- 1 to 2 tablespoons nutritional yeast (use the larger amount for a cheesier flavor)
- 1 medium clove garlic, minced
- 1/2 teaspoon sea salt, or to taste
- 1/4 teaspoon ground black pepper

Cut the bell pepper in half, remove the stems and seeds, and arrange on a foil-lined baking sheet. Broil on high heat until the pepper is slightly blackened and charred. Alternatively, the bell pepper can be lightly blackened directly over a gas flame or charred on a BBQ grill. After the pepper is charred, you can leave the skin on like I do, or transfer it to a bowl and cover with plastic wrap for about 5 minutes to let the skin soften for easy removal with your fingers.

Transfer the roasted red pepper to a blender or food processor. Add the cashews, lemon juice, 2 tablespoons of water, miso, dates (if using), nutritional yeast, garlic, salt, and pepper. Blend until smooth and creamy. If the dressing seems too thick, or is difficult to blend, add more water, 1 tablespoon at a time, until the desired consistency is achieved.

MAKES ABOUT 1 CUP

Tahini Cream Salad Dressing

This dressing is delicious and so simple to make. I love the short ingredient list and how quickly I can whip it up at a moment's notice. I use this recipe not just for salads, but everywhere: as a dip for freshly cut raw vegetables; drizzled over soups, vegan omelets, baked russet or sweet potatoes, and more.

1/2 cup plain unsweetened soymilk
1/4 cup tahini
1/4 cup fresh or bottled lemon juice
1 teaspoon ground golden flaxseed
1/2 teaspoon sea salt, or to taste
A pinch of ground black pepper

In a blender, combine the soymilk, tahini, lemon juice, flaxseed, salt, and pepper. Blend until completely smooth and creamy, about 1 minute.

MAKES ABOUT 1 CUP

Creamy Sesame Dressing

Use this dressing on the Asian Cabbage Salad with Wasabi Chickpeas and Oranges on page 98.

1/4 cup Date Paste (page 16)
2 tablespoons coconut butter
2 tablespoons rice vinegar
2 to 3 tablespoons tamari or Bragg Liquid Aminos
1/4 cup unsweetened soy milk

1 small clove garlic, minced
Pinch of red pepper flakes
1 teaspoon finely minced fresh ginger
1/4 teaspoon ground black pepper
2 tablespoons sesame seeds (regular or black)

In a blender, combine the date paste, coconut butter, vinegar, tamari, soy milk, garlic, red pepper flakes, ginger, and pepper. Blend until completely smooth and creamy. Add the sesame seeds and pulse gently to distribute, leaving the sesame seeds whole.

MAKES ABOUT 1 CUP

Creamy Vegan Ranch Dressing

If you don't have a high-speed blender, you may want to soak the cashews for a few hours before blending.

- 3/4 cup unsweetened soy milk
- 1/2 cup raw cashew pieces
- 1 tablespoon apple cider vinegar
- 1 teaspoon nutritional yeast
- 1/2 teaspoon garlic powder
- 1/2 teaspoon onion powder
- 1/2 teaspoon sea salt, or to taste
- 1/4 teaspoon ground black pepper
- 1 teaspoon dried dill
- 1 teaspoon dried parsley
- 1 tablespoon snipped fresh or dried chives

In a blender, combine the soy milk, cashews, vinegar, nutritional yeast, garlic powder, onion powder, salt, and pepper. Blend until completely smooth and creamy, 1 to 2 minutes. Add the dill, parsley, and chives and pulse just to combine.

MAKES ABOUT 1 1/4 CUPS

Rich Balsamic Vinaigrette

If you don't have a high-speed blender, you may want to soak the dates for a few hours in warm water before blending. This dressing is used in the Greek Chickpea Chopped Salad on page 106.

- 1/2 cup water
- 1/4 cup red wine vinegar
- 1/4 cup balsamic vinegar
- 4 pitted, chopped soft medjool dates (or 4 tablespoons date paste)
- 4 small cloves garlic, minced
- 1 tablespoon almond butter or tahini
- 1 teaspoon dried oregano
- 1 teaspoon dried basil
- 1/2 teaspoon onion powder
- 1/2 teaspoon sea salt, or to taste
- 1/2 teaspoon ground black pepper

In a blender, combine the water, red wine vinegar, balsamic vinegar, dates, garlic, almond butter, oregano, basil, onion powder, salt, and pepper. Blend all of the ingredients until smooth and creamy, about 1 minute.

MAKES ABOUT 1 1/4 CUPS

Spicy Caesar Dressing

This delicious vegan version of the classic Caesar salad dressing has all the feisty kick of the original with none of the fat that comes with the traditional oil, egg, dairy, and anchovy-based dressing.

1/2 cup extra-firm silken tofu, drained and patted dry (about 4 ounces)
1/4 cup raw cashew pieces, raw pine nuts, or slivered blanched almonds
1 tablespoon nutritional yeast
2 tablespoons apple cider vinegar
1 tablespoon lemon juice
1 tablespoon tamari or Bragg Liquid Aminos
1/3 cup unsweetened almond milk
1 teaspoon capers
2 large cloves garlic, minced
1 teaspoon Dijon mustard
1 to 2 teaspoons ground black pepper (I like 2 for an extra-spicy kick)
1 teaspoon sea salt, or to taste

In a blender, combine the tofu, cashews, nutritional yeast, vinegar, lemon juice, tamari, almond milk, capers, garlic, mustard, pepper, and salt. Blend all of the ingredients until smooth and creamy, about 1 minute.

MAKES ABOUT 1 1/2 CUPS

Oil-Free Goddess Dressing

Store-bought "goddess" dressings are simply divine, which is probably why they are named after a female deity! This version is lower in fat and calories than the original while still being rich, creamy, and delicious.

1/4 cup tahini
1/4 cup apple cider vinegar
1/4 cup tamari or Bragg Liquid Aminos
1 tablespoon lemon juice
1/2 teaspoon garlic powder
1/4 teaspoon onion powder
1 teaspoon dried parsley
1/2 cup plain unsweetened soymilk
1 teaspoon ground golden flaxseed
1/2 teaspoon sea salt, or to taste
1/4 teaspoon ground black pepper

In a blender, combine the tahini, vinegar, tamari, lemon juice, garlic powder, onion powder, parsley, soymilk, flaxseed, salt, and pepper. Blend until smooth and creamy, about 1 minute.

MAKES ABOUT 1 1/4 CUPS

Super-Tasty Special Sauce

This dressing is inspired by one that I saw on Instagram that was made with a simple combination of Vegenaise, Bragg Liquid Aminos, and nutritional yeast mixed with water. In this recipe I'm switching things up to reduce the fat and oil content using my Cashew Sour Cream instead of the mayo. I love the flavor of this dressing so much I could drink it! So be warned, it is addictive—you'll want to pour it on everything.

2/3 cup Cashew Sour Cream (page 154)
2 tablespoons nutritional yeast
2 tablespoons tamari or Bragg Liquid Aminos
2 to 4 tablespoons water

In a glass jar with a tight-fitting lid, combine the Cashew Sour Cream, nutritional yeast, tamari, and 2 tablespoons of water. Put the lid on the jar and shake vigorously to combine. Add additional water, if needed.

MAKES ABOUT 1 CUP

Main Event Salads

These salads are intended to be used as a main course. They are hearty and filling enough to break that "just a salad" stigma. Eating one of these monster-sized salads most days is a key to success for *The Abundance Diet*.

Hearty Vegetable Pasta Salad

This is the perfect pasta salad for summertime, and it is great for using up veggies in the fridge! The ones I've listed here are just a guideline, so feel free to substitute any of your favorites or what you have on hand. If desired, this pasta salad can be served over a bed of lettuce. **Note:** For the pasta, I used fusilli, cooked until al dente for 8 to 9 minutes, in boiling salted water, then drained and rinsed under cold water.

8 ounces cooked brown rice pasta (see Note)
1 (15.5-ounce) can kidney beans, drained and rinsed (or 1 1/2 cups thawed frozen peas)
1 cup broccoli florets, cut into bite-sized pieces
2 medium carrots, cut into 1/2-inch dice
2 Roma tomatoes, cut into 1/2-inch dice
3/4 cup diced cucumber
1 rib celery, cut into 1/4-inch dice
12 pitted olives (your favorite variety), thinly sliced
2/3 cup Rich Balsamic Vinaigrette (page 92)
1/4 teaspoon sea salt, or to taste
1/8 teaspoon ground black pepper, or to taste

In a large bowl, combine the pasta, beans, broccoli, carrots, tomatoes, cucumber, celery, and olives. Pour the dressing over the salad and toss gently to coat. Season with salt and pepper.

MAKES 4 SERVINGS

Asian Cabbage Salad with Wasabi Chickpeas and Oranges

This recipe reminds me of the "Asian-inspired" salads that you can get at many chain restaurants. I was surprised to find out that a salad I thought was relatively healthy could pack over 1,000 calories and be fully loaded with fat and sugar. In this version, I've used cabbage instead of lettuce for extra crunch and lightened up the toppings and dressing. If you prefer lettuce over cabbage, go ahead and swap your favorite head of lettuce for the green cabbage.

> 4 navel oranges, supremed (instructions below)
> 1 small head green cabbage, cut into 1/4 inch thin ribbons
> 1/4 small head purple cabbage, cut into 1/4 inch thin ribbons
> 3 medium carrots, shredded
> 1 recipe Wasabi Chickpeas (page 152) or 1 1/2 cups shelled edamame
>   (for a quicker version)
> Creamy Sesame Dressing (page 89)
> 1/4 cup roughly chopped cilantro, for garnish
> 2 tablespoons sesame seeds, for garnish (optional)

In a large salad bowl, combine the oranges, green cabbage, purple cabbage, carrots, and wasabi chickpeas. Gently toss the salad to combine. Pour the dressing over the salad and gently toss again until the dressing completely coats the ingredients. Divide the cabbage salad among four large salad plates, then garnish with cilantro and the sesame seeds, if using.

MAKES 4 SERVINGS

How to Supreme an Orange

Cut off the stem end and bottom end of each orange. You want to cut deep enough to reveal the orange fruit inside, but not so deep that you waste the fruit. Set the fruit down on one of its cut sides, then cut away the peel in strips, following the curve of the orange and wasting as little fruit as possible, rotating and cutting until all of the peel is cut away. Then, using your knife, cut the segments of the orange away from the core, leaving the membranes behind. This method takes all of the bitterness out of an orange while wasting very little fruit.

Curried Brown Rice Salad

This super-yummy whole grain salad is full of beautiful flavors and textures. It gets gobbled up at parties and potlucks. My home crowd and recipe testers adored it too. Try serving it over a bed of baby greens for a lovely presentation.

Note: This salad can be made with an equal amount of quinoa instead of the brown rice.

SALAD
4 cups cooked and cooled brown basmati or brown jasmine rice
6 large celery ribs, cut into 1/4-inch dice
1 small bunch green onions, cut into 1/4-inch pieces
2 large carrots, cut into 1/2-inch dice or matchsticks
1 medium red bell pepper, cut into 1/2-inch dice
1/2 cup finely chopped cilantro
1/4 cup raw cashews, roughly chopped
1/4 cup dried cranberries or golden raisins

DRESSING
3 tablespoons white wine vinegar
2 teaspoons red curry powder, or to taste (I used Patak's brand)
1 teaspoon ground cumin
1/2 teaspoon ground ginger
1/2 teaspoon garlic powder
1/3 cup Date Paste (page 16)
1 tablespoon almond butter
1/2 teaspoon sea salt, or to taste
1/8 teaspoon ground black pepper

In a large bowl, combine the rice, celery, green onion, carrots, bell pepper, cilantro, cashews, and cranberries. Toss until well mixed. Set aside.

In a small bowl, combine the vinegar, curry powder, cumin, ginger, garlic powder, date paste, almond butter, salt, and pepper. Stir with a wire whisk until combined. Pour the dressing over the salad and toss to combine. Serve at room temperature.

MAKES 4 SERVINGS

Black Bean Veggie Burger Salad with Avocado Ranch Dressing

My favorite veggie burger is made with black beans and a hefty portion of guacamole. I've recreated that dish here as a delicious salad.

VEGGIE BURGERS

1 (15.5-ounce) can black beans, drained and rinsed

1/4 cup instant oats (certified gluten-free if necessary)

2 tablespoons masa harina or chickpea flour

1/4 cup finely minced red onion

1 teaspoon ground cumin

1 tablespoon nutritional yeast

1 teaspoon sriracha or other hot sauce

1 clove minced garlic

1 tablespoon ground golden flax seeds

1/2 small jalapeño, finely minced, seeds (remove ribs for less heat)

2 tablespoons roughly chopped cilantro

1 teaspoon sea salt (or to taste)

2 to 3 tablespoons water, or as needed

In a food processor, combine the black beans, oats, masa harina, onion, cumin, nutritional yeast, sriracha, garlic, flaxseed, jalapeño, cilantro, and salt. Process until the ingredients are roughly combined. Add 2 tablespoons of water and pulse until the mixture becomes more cohesive. Use an additional tablespoon or two of water if necessary to get the mixture to stick together. Divide the burger mixture into 4 thick patties or into twelve 1-inch rounds or balls (depending on your preference). Cook the burgers for 4 to 6 minutes per side in a large nonstick skillet over medium heat. Cook the rounds for 2 to 3 minutes per side.

SALAD AND DRESSING

1 recipe Creamy Vegan Ranch Dressing (page 91)

1 large Hass avocado, peeled, pitted, and quartered

1 large head green leaf lettuce, washed and torn into bite-sized pieces

1 cup shredded purple cabbage

1/2 cup shredded carrots

2 Roma tomatoes, sliced

1/2 small red onion, sliced into 1/4 inch rings (about 1/4 cup)

In a blender, combine the prepared Creamy Vegan Ranch dressing and the avocado. Blend for 30 to 60 seconds until completely smooth and creamy.

Assembly: Layer the lettuce, cabbage, carrots, tomatoes, and onion rings on four dinner plates. Top each salad with one of the veggie burgers (you can crumble the veggie burger over the salad if you like). Drizzle the dressing over the top just before serving.

MAKES 4 SERVINGS

Notes: For bite-sized veggie burgers use a small cookie scoop and form the mixture into 1-inch rounds instead of thick patties. You should get about 12 rounds. Cook the rounds for 2 to 3 minutes per side in a large nonstick skillet over medium heat. Divide the veggie burger bites per salad.

Chipotle Knock-Off Chopped Salad

I adore the salads at Chipotle, but let's face it, even the veggie-only options can turn one into a gigantic calorie bomb with all the variable toppings you can choose from. I've recreated a quick-chop version of the salad that is still very hearty and filling, but with a much lower calorie count.

    1 large head romaine lettuce, washed, dried and cut into 1 inch pieces
    1 (15.5-ounce) can pinto beans or black beans, drained and rinsed
    1/2 teaspoon onion powder
    1/2 teaspoon liquid smoke
    Dash of chipotle powder
    2 cups cooked brown rice
    Juice of 1 large lime
    1/4 cup roughly chopped cilantro
    1 large Hass avocado, peeled, pitted, and cut into 1/2 inch dice
    1 cup fresh or frozen corn, thawed if frozen
    Fire-Roasted Salsa (page 155)
    Cashew Sour Cream (page 154)
    Oil-Free Chipotle Knock-Off Dressing (recipe follows)

In a large bowl, combine the lettuce and beans. Sprinkle with the onion powder and liquid smoke. Toss to combine. Add the cooked rice, then drizzle with the lime juice and add the cilantro. Toss again to combine. Add the avocado and corn and toss the salad gently. Divide the chopped salad onto four large dinner plates or into four large soup bowls and top each servings with the corn and salsa and a dollop of sour cream. Drizzle each salad with the dressing.

MAKES 4 SERVINGS

Note: This is meant to be a cold salad, but if you prefer a salad with warmed elements like Chipotle restaurant offers, feel free to warm the beans, rice, and corn before adding them to the salad.

Oil-Free Chipotle Knock-Off Dressing

3 tablespoons red wine vinegar
1/2 cup unsweetened applesauce
2 tablespoons agave or pure maple syrup
1 tablespoon almond butter or 2 tablespoons raw cashew pieces
3 tablespoons water
1/2 teaspoon ground cumin
1/2 teaspoon chili powder
1/2 teaspoon dried oregano
Dash of ground chipotle powder
1/2 teaspoon sea salt, or to taste

In a blender, combine the vinegar, applesauce, agave, almond butter, water, cumin, chili powder, oregano, chipotle powder, and salt. Blend until completely smooth and creamy, about 1 minute.

MAKES ABOUT 1 CUP

Falafel Salad with Quinoa Tabbouleh

Falafel is one of my absolute favorite foods! I fell in love with it when I was living in Australia and the kebab vendors always had fantastic falafel kebabs. This falafel is made using non-traditional methods. I've used chickpea flour instead of the dried bean to save time, and these are baked rather than fried, which makes them both filling and light in calories.

FALAFEL

1 cup chickpea flour (besan)
1 tablespoon ground golden flaxseed
1 teaspoon ground cumin
1/2 teaspoon ground coriander
1/2 teaspoon smoked paprika
1/2 teaspoon sea salt (or to taste)
1/4 teaspoon ground black pepper
Dash of cayenne
1/4 teaspoon baking soda
1 large garlic clove, finely minced
1 small yellow onion, finely minced
1/4 cup finely chopped parsley
1/4 cup finely chopped cilantro
1 tablespoon lemon juice
1/4 to 1/3 cup water, as needed

QUINOA TABBOULEH

1 1/4 cups water
3/4 cup quinoa, rinsed well and drained
1 clove garlic, minced
1 small cucumber, cut into 1/4-inch dice
2 Roma tomatoes, cut into 1/4-inch dice
1/2 teaspoon sea salt, or to taste
1 cup finely chopped parsley
1/4 cup finely chopped fresh mint
2 to 3 tablespoons fresh lemon juice

ASSEMBLY

1 large head red leaf lettuce, washed and torn into bite-sized pieces
1/2 small purple onion, cut into rings (about 1/4 cup)
1 recipe Tahini Cream Salad Dressing (page 89)

Falafel: Preheat the oven to 375°F. In a medium bowl, whisk together the chickpea flour, flaxseed, cumin, coriander, paprika, salt, black pepper, and baking soda. Add the garlic, onion, parsley, and cilantro, and stir to coat all of the ingredients. Add the lemon juice and 1/3 cup of the water, adding more water, 1 tablespoon at a time, if necessary. Let the batter rest for 10 to 15 minutes. Shape the dough into 1-inch balls using a small ice cream or cookie scoop. If you find the dough too sticky, use wet hands to shape the dough into balls. Arrange the falafel on a baking sheet lined with parchment paper or a Silpat baking mat. Spray them with a quick burst of pan spray to help them brown. Bake the falafels for 20 to 25 minutes, or until golden and cooked through. While the falafel is cooking, prepare the tabbouleh.

Quinoa Tabbouleh: Bring the water to a boil in a small lidded saucepan and add the quinoa. Return the water to a boil and then reduce heat to medium-low. Cover the saucepan with the lid and simmer for 15 minutes. Remove the quinoa from the heat. It should still have a fair bit of toothy bite, as it will absorb more liquid from the vegetables, so don't worry if it feels firmer than you normally prepare it. Cool the quinoa by rinsing it under cold water and thoroughly draining, or by letting it chill in the fridge for 30 to 60 minutes. In a large bowl, combine the chilled quinoa with the garlic, cucumber, tomatoes, salt, parsley, mint, and lemon juice.

Assembly: Divide the lettuce, tabbouleh, and onion among four large salad plates. Top each salad with an even number of the falafel. Drizzle the tahini cream salad dressing over the top of the salads.

MAKES 4 SERVINGS

Note: For a lighter and faster dish, replace the Quinoa Tabbouleh with the Cauliflower or Parsnip Tabbouleh (page 120).

Greek Chickpea Chopped Salad

There's something about Greek salad that is universally appealing. The salty bite of the olives and feta, the delicious tang of the vinaigrette dressing married to the savory bite of onion, crisp lettuce, cool cucumber, and fresh tomato just put me in a super happy place. I love this version as a chop salad that includes chickpeas for added protein, nutrition, and toothy bite. I've created a tofu feta recipe to help satisfy any dairy cravings you may be having. (For best results, make the tofu feta a day in advance.)

1 large head romaine lettuce, washed and torn into bite-sized pieces
1 cup canned chickpeas, drained and rinsed
1/2 cup chopped red onion
4 Roma tomatoes, cut into 1/2-inch dice
1 large cucumber, cut into 1/2-inch dice
12 pitted Kalamata olives, thinly sliced
Tofu Feta (recipe follows)
1 recipe Rich Balsamic Vinaigrette (page 92)
Sea salt and ground black pepper, to taste

In a large bowl, combine the lettuce, chickpeas, red onion, tomatoes, and cucumber. Toss gently to combine. Transfer the salad to large salad plates or bowls. Top each salad with the crumbled Tofu Feta and drizzle with the Rich Balsamic Vinaigrette. Season with salt and pepper to taste, if desired.

MAKES 4 SERVINGS

Tofu Feta

1 (14-ounce) block extra-firm tofu, drained and blotted dry
3 tablespoons fresh or bottled lemon juice
1/2 teaspoon sea salt, or to taste

Press the tofu for several hours or overnight to remove as much excess water as possible. Roughly crumble the pressed tofu into a medium-sized bowl. Drizzle the tofu with the lemon juice and sprinkle with salt. Toss gently to combine. Refrigerate the tofu overnight for the best flavor.

Pressing Tofu

In order to remove excess liquid, tofu needs to be pressed. This makes the tofu firmer and allows it to more easily absorb marinades and flavors. I use a Tofu Xpress, which is a top-of-the-line tofu press. It presses tofu quickly and efficiently.

You can press tofu without a manufactured press. To do so, you'll need a sturdy kitchen plate, four clean lint-free kitchen towels and a heavy object such as a cast iron skillet or several hardbound books. To press the tofu, place two of the towels on the kitchen plate. Place the drained and blotted tofu onto the towels on the plate. Cover the tofu with the remaining two towels and then it weight down with your heavy object. This process takes about 30 minutes. The towels will absorb the excess liquid and the tofu will be ready to use in your recipe.

Lentil Taco Salad
with Roasted Red Pepper Dressing

While you might think a taco salad is a good choice at a restaurant, you may be shocked to find that it is one of the most calorie- and fat-dense items on the menu. This taco salad made with lentils, however, is so yummy and indulgent, you'll wonder whether you're really eating "diet food." It is also delicious served with the Creamy Vegan Ranch Dressing (page 91).

LENTIL TACO "MEAT"

1/4 cup vegetable broth

1 cup chopped yellow or white onion

1 large carrot, cut into 1/4-inch dice

1 large bell pepper (red or green), cut into 1/2-inch dice

1 cup dried brown or green lentils, sorted and well rinsed

2 cups vegetable broth

2 tablespoons chili powder

1 tablespoon ground cumin

2 teaspoons dried oregano

1/4 cup tomato paste

1 garlic clove, minced

1 tablespoon nutritional yeast

1 tablespoon tamari or Bragg Liquid Aminos

1/2 teaspoons sea salt, or to taste

1/4 teaspoon ground black pepper

1 tablespoon almond butter or tahini

1/2 cup roughly chopped cilantro

SALAD

1 large head romaine lettuce, washed and torn into bite-sized pieces

1/4 head purple cabbage, cut into 1/4-inch ribbons

2 Roma tomatoes, cut into 1/4-inch dice

1 medium carrot, shredded

Cashew Sour Cream (page 154)

Fire-Roasted Salsa (page 155)

Roasted Red Pepper Dressing, (page 88)

2 ounces low- or no-oil baked corn chips, for topping (crushed, if desired)

Heat the broth in a medium lidded saucepan over medium-high heat. Add the onion and sauté for 1 to 2 minutes. Add the carrot and bell pepper and sauté until the onion is translucent, about 5 minutes. Add the lentils, vegetable broth, chili powder, cumin, oregano, tomato paste, garlic, nutritional yeast, and tamari, and bring to a boil, stirring occasionally. Cover, reduce the heat to medium-low, and simmer for 45 to 60 minutes until all liquid is absorbed. Taste for seasonings and add salt and pepper, if desired. Stir in the almond butter and cilantro. Set aside.

Divide the lettuce, cabbage, tomato, and carrots among four large plates. Top with the lentil taco "meat" and dollops of the sour cream and salsa. Drizzle with the salad dressing and a sprinkling of corn chips.

MAKES 4 SERVINGS

Green Goddess Spinach Salad

We all need food that makes us feel empowered, vibrant, and in control of our health. This salad meets all of those requirements and then some. Share it with someone you love for the ultimate blissful salad experience.

1 small clove garlic, cut in half
10 ounces fresh baby spinach
3/4 cup Oil-Free Goddess Dressing (page 94)
1 (14-ounce) can artichoke hearts, drained and rinsed
2 Roma tomatoes, cut lengthwise into 8 wedges each
2 medium carrots, cut into 2-inch matchsticks
1/2 recipe Tofu Feta (page 106)
1 large Hass avocado, peeled, pitted, and cut into 1/2-inch slices
1/4 cup chopped red onion
1/4 cup dried cranberries
4 tablespoons toasted slivered almonds
Sea salt and black pepper, to taste (optional)

Using the cut half of the garlic, rub the interior of a large salad bowl all over until it is fragrant. Save the garlic for another use. Transfer the spinach to the bowl. Pour the dressing over the spinach and toss to coat completely. Divide the dressed spinach among four large salad plates. Arrange the artichoke hearts, tomatoes, carrots, Tofu Feta, avocado, cranberries, red onion, and slivered almonds evenly over the spinach. Season with salt and pepper to taste, if desired.

MAKES 4 SERVINGS

Variation: In cold weather, this salad is delicious served warm as a wilted salad. Increase the spinach to 16 ounces and follow these directions: Add the artichoke hearts, tomatoes, carrots, red onion and garlic (minced this time) to a large skillet with 1/4 cup of vegetable broth and sauté until the onions are soft, 3 to 5 minutes. Add the spinach a big handful at a time, stirring after each addition, until it is just barely wilted. Divide the wilted vegetables among four plates. Divide the Oil-Free Goddess Dressing over the salads and arrange the Tofu Feta, cranberries, avocado, and slivered toasted almonds over the salad. Season with salt and pepper if desired.

Rawkin' Rainbow Kale Salad with Creamy Chili-Lime Dressing

I call this "a salad for the kale haters" because my husband, who isn't fond of kale when it isn't a kale chip or well hidden in a smoothie, asked for seconds on this incredibly lush and dreamy salad.

CREAMY CHILI LIME DRESSING

1 large red bell pepper, cut into 1-inch pieces

1 large clove garlic, minced

1/4 cup raw cashew pieces (soaked for 4 to 6 hours

1 tablespoon tamari or Bragg Liquid Aminos

Juice of 1 large lime

1 teaspoon chili powder, or more (depending on your heat preference)

1 teaspoon ground cumin

Dash of cayenne

1/2 teaspoon sea salt, or to taste

1/8 teaspoon ground black pepper

RAINBOW KALE SALAD

1 large bunch (16 ounces) lacinato or dinosaur kale, tough stems removed, then cut into 1/4-inch shreds

1/2 cup finely chopped cilantro

1/4 head small purple cabbage, cut into 1/4-inch ribbons

1/2 cup red onion, cut into 1/4-inch dice or thinly sliced rings

1 large carrot, cut into thin 2-inch long matchsticks

1 large ripe Hass avocado, peeled, pitted, and cut into 1/2-inch cubes

1 small jicama, cut into 2-inch long matchsticks

Salt and ground black pepper, to taste

Lime wedges, for serving (optional)

In a high-speed blender or a food processor, combine the red bell pepper, garlic, cashews, tamari, lime juice, chili powder, cumin, cayenne, salt, and pepper. Blend until completely smooth and creamy, 1 to 2 minutes.

Transfer the kale and the cilantro to a large salad bowl and pour on the dressing. Toss until all the kale is thoroughly coated, then massage the kale with your hands for 1 to 2 minutes. (Massaging kale makes it taste better!) Divide the kale salad among four large plates and top with the purple cabbage, red onion, carrot, avocado, and jicama. Season with a bit of salt and pepper and serve with lime wedges, if desired.

MAKES 4 SERVINGS

The Ultimate Lentil Salad

My friend Amanda brought me this salad one day for lunch. It has become one of my favorite salads of all time. This adaptation is oil-free and calorie-wise, yet it's fancy enough to serve at a dinner party! The colors are gorgeous and the flavor has an incredible vibrant pop. Don't let the spice list in the dressing scare you; each spice adds a delicate nuance of flavor. This is lovely served over a bed of spinach or your favorite greens.

SALAD
- 1 1/4 cups dry French green lentils
- 1 medium red onion, cut into 1/4-inch dice
- 1/4 cup currants
- 2 tablespoons capers
- 1 cup diced radishes
- 1 cup diced carrots
- 1/4 cup roughly chopped pecans
- 1/2 cup roughly chopped fresh basil

DRESSING
- 3 tablespoons Date Paste (page 16)
- 3 tablespoons apple cider vinegar
- 2 teaspoons Dijon mustard
- 1 tablespoon tahini
- 1/2 teaspoon ground cumin
- 1/4 teaspoon turmeric
- 1/4 teaspoon ground coriander
- 1/4 teaspoon ground cardamom
- Dash of cayenne
- 1/8 teaspoon ground cloves
- 1/8 teaspoon ground nutmeg
- 1/8 teaspoon ground cinnamon
- 3/4 teaspoon sea salt
- 1/2 teaspoon ground black pepper

Cook the lentils a saucepan in 2 cups of salted water, simmering for 20 to 25 minutes. You want the lentils to keep their toothy bite and not to be mushy, so don't overcook. Rinse the lentils in cool water or refrigerate them for 60 minutes before proceeding with the recipe.

In a large salad bowl, combine the cooked and cooled lentils, onion, currants, capers, radishes, carrots, pecans, and basil. Set aside.

In a small bowl, whisk together the Date Paste, vinegar, mustard, tahini, cumin, turmeric, coriander, cardamom, cayenne, cloves, nutmeg, cinnamon, salt, and pepper, whisking until thoroughly combined.

Pour the dressing over the lentil salad and toss a few times to allow the ingredients to marry. This salad can be served straight away at room temperature, or refrigerated for a few hours to marinate.

MAKES 4 SERVINGS

Vegan Egg Salad over Baby Greens with Cheesy Crackers

Our family used to love traditional egg salad, but now we don't eat eggs and don't want to add cholesterol to our diets. It has been a challenge to figure out how to make a convincing vegan egg salad taste just right, but I think this recipe cracks the code. Plus, you get to serve it over a bed of baby greens and eat it with crunchy cheesy crackers for the win! One of the secrets to the success of this salad lies in the use of kala namak (black salt). This salt is actually pinkish in color. It has the pungent sulfury smell and taste reminiscent of eggs. You can find kala namak at Indian grocers or online. However, if you can't locate it, you can simply substitute fine sea salt, but the end result won't taste as eggy.

1 small potato (about 4 ounces)
1 tablespoon nutritional yeast
1/2 teaspoon kala namak (black salt)
1/4 teaspoon ground turmeric
1/2 teaspoon ground mustard powder
1 cup Cashew Sour Cream (page 154), divided
14 ounces extra-firm tofu, drained and blotted dry, cut into 1/2-inch cubes
1 tablespoon fresh or dried chives
1 teaspoon dried dill
1 teaspoon to 1 tablespoon dill pickle relish (to taste)
Salt and ground black pepper, to taste (optional)
8 ounces baby greens
1 recipe Cheesy Gluten-Free Crackers (page 156)
Vegetables for garnish (radish, carrot, cucumber, etc.)

Boil the potato until tender. Or, to save time, microwave the potato for a few minutes. Cool the potato and peel it, then transfer it to a medium-sized bowl and mash it with a fork until it's finely mashed. Add the nutritional yeast, kala namak, turmeric, mustard powder, and 2 tablespoons of the sour cream. Mash and stir the mixture until the ingredients are well combined. Add the cubed tofu and the remaining sour cream to the bowl, stirring gently. Fold in the chives, dill, and relish. Season with salt and pepper to taste, if desired. Serve over a bed of baby greens with the cheesy crackers and vegetable garnishes of your choice.

MAKES 4 SERVINGS

Niçoise Salad with Smoky Tofu and Creamy Miso Dressing

Something about eating Niçoise salad just feels fancy. Perhaps it's because of the French origins of the recipe, or perhaps it's the cute little potatoes and the beautiful long French green beans. Traditional Niçoise salad contains tuna, eggs, and anchovies and is dressed with an oil-based vinaigrette. I replace the tuna and eggs here with a gorgeous smoky tofu recipe that I think you'll adore. The dressing is dreamy, creamy, and completely non-traditional. (See photo on page vi.)

SMOKY TOFU
1 (14-ounce) package extra-firm tofu, drained and blotted dry
2 tablespoons tamari or Bragg Liquid Aminos
1 small clove garlic, minced
1 tablespoon mirin
1/2 tablespoon pure maple syrup
1/2 tablespoon tomato paste (optional, for a richer marinade)
1 teaspoon liquid smoke
1/2 teaspoon nutritional yeast
1/2 teaspoon toasted sesame oil
1/4 teaspoon sea salt (or to taste)
1/4 teaspoon ground black pepper

Press the tofu (see page 109) for 30 minutes or longer to release the extra liquid. Cut the tofu into 1-inch cubes and set aside.

In a medium bowl, combine the tamari, garlic, mirin, maple syrup, tomato paste (if using), liquid smoke, nutritional yeast, sesame oil, salt, and pepper. Whisk to blend well. Add the tofu to the bowl and gently toss to coat. Let the tofu absorb the marinade for 5 to 10 minutes.

Heat a large nonstick skillet over medium-high heat. Add the tofu and cook for 4 minutes on each side until golden and slightly crispy. Set aside.

SALAD
16 ounces baby red or baby Yukon gold potatoes
16 ounces slender green beans, ends trimmed
2 heads Bibb or butter lettuce, torn into bite-sized pieces
2 large Roma tomatoes, cut into 1/2-inch slices

1/2 cup brine-cured, pitted olives (green or black or a combination of both)

1/2 medium red onion, sliced into 1/4-inch rings

1/2 cup roughly chopped fresh herbs (I like parsley, tarragon, chives, or rosemary, or a combination)

In a medium pot, bring 6 cups of salted water to a boil. Add the potatoes and boil for 2 minutes at a rolling boil. Add the green beans to the water and boil for 4 to 6 minutes longer or until the potatoes and the green beans are fork-tender. Drain the vegetables and set aside to cool.

CREAMY MISO DRESSING

1/2 cup unsweetened soy milk

2 tablespoons mellow white miso

1 small clove garlic, minced

1/2 tablespoon ground golden flaxseed

1 tablespoon fresh lemon juice

1 tablespoon white wine vinegar

1 tablespoon Dijon mustard

1 tablespoon almond butter or tahini

1 1/2 tablespoons minced shallots or sweet onion

2 teaspoons capers, drained and roughly chopped

1 tablespoon tamari or Bragg Liquid Aminos

1/2 teaspoon sea salt, or to taste

1/8 teaspoon ground black pepper

In a blender, combine the soy milk, miso, garlic, flaxseed, lemon juice, vinegar, mustard, almond butter, shallots, capers, tamari, salt, and pepper. Blend until completely smooth and creamy, about 1 minute. The dressing will thicken more when refrigerated.

Assembly: Portion out the smoky tofu, potatoes, green beans, lettuce, tomatoes olives and onions among four large plates. Sprinkle with fresh herbs if desired. Serve each salad with about 1/4 cup of the dressing on the side for dipping or pouring over.

Note: If you prefer Niçoise with a vinaigrette-type dressing, feel free to use the Rich Balsamic Vinaigrette (page 92) instead. Some of my testers also enjoyed this salad with the Spicy Caesar Dressing (page 93).

MAKES 4 SERVINGS

Lighter Salads

These salads are great for a side dish to round out any of the soups or main dish meals. They are also a great pick-me-up light meal for that afternoon slump.

Broccoli, Grape, and Spinach Salad

This salad is famous at a few restaurants and delis in my neck of the woods. It's not hard to see why! There is a perfect combination of crunchy, savory, sweet, and tart all in one salad. Even kids love it. As a small side, this salad can be a calorie bomb with a full-fat mayo-based dressing, so I use the delicious Creamy Raspberry Poppy Seed Dressing instead.

> **1 small head broccoli, separated into tiny bite-sized florets**
> **2 cups red grapes, halved**
> **8 ounces fresh baby spinach**
> **1/2 cup Creamy Raspberry Poppy Seed Dressing (page 87)**
> **Sea salt and ground black pepper, to taste (optional)**

In a large salad bowl, combine the broccoli, grapes, and spinach and toss to combine. Drizzle the dressing over the salad and toss until all of the ingredients are coated. Taste for seasoning and add salt and pepper, if desired.

MAKES 4 SERVINGS

Note: if you like a creamier salad dressing, add a couple of tablespoons of Cashew Sour Cream (page 154) to the dressing before drizzling over the salad.

Carrot Ribbon Salad
with Pepita Maple Butter Dressing

This salad has one of the prettiest presentations out of all the recipes in the book. The vibrant orange carrot ribbons contrast beautifully with the cranberries and the pale green dressing. It tastes every bit as good as it looks.

- 12 large carrots, shaved into thin ribbons with a vegetable peeler, cut into matchsticks, or spiraled with a spiralizer
- 2 tablespoons pepita (pumpkin seed) butter (see Note)
- 1 tablespoon pure maple syrup
- 1 tablespoon Date Paste (page 16)
- 1 tablespoon tamari or Bragg Liquid Aminos
- 1/4 cup unsweetened almond milk
- 1 tablespoon white wine vinegar
- 1/2 tablespoon nutritional yeast (optional)
- 1 small clove garlic, minced
- 1/4 teaspoon sea salt
- 1/4 cup raw pepitas (pumpkin seeds)
- 1/4 cup dried cranberries or golden raisins

Arrange the carrots on four salad plates; pile them high! Set aside.

In a small bowl, whisk together the pumpkin seed butter, maple syrup, Date Paste, tamari, almond milk, vinegar, nutritional yeast, garlic, and salt. Whisk until all of the ingredients are emulsified.

Drizzle the dressing onto the salads, then sprinkle with the pepita seeds and cranberries.

MAKES 4 SERVINGS

Note: Pepita butter can be difficult to find, but it is worth making yourself. I make mine by blending pepita seeds in my Blendtec Twister Jar. It keeps for a very long time in the refrigerator and is handy to have on hand for when you want to whip up a batch of this dressing, which is delicious on any salad. Alternatively, you can make this dressing in a high-speed blender with whole pepita seeds. You'll need to double the amount of pepita seeds, since 2 tablespoons of pepita seeds butter is equal to 1/4 cup pepita seeds. You may also want to consider doubling the ingredients for better blending. For a simpler variation, substitute almond butter for the pepita butter in the salad dressing.

Cauliflower or Parsnip Tabbouleh

This tabbouleh is light, refreshing, and grain-free. You can use it as a pick-me-up in the afternoon or for a lower-calorie version of the Quinoa Tabbouleh in the salad on page 104. This recipe is best eaten the day it is made.

1 small head cauliflower, separated into small florets, or
    6 parsnips cut into 1-inch dice
1 clove garlic, finely minced
1 small cucumber, cut into 1/4-inch dice
2 Roma tomatoes, cut into 1/2-inch dice
1 cup finely chopped parsley
1/4 cup finely chopped fresh mint
2 to 3 tablespoons fresh lemon juice
1/2 teaspoon sea salt, or to taste

Place the cauliflower in a food processor and pulse until the pieces are very fine and resemble rice or bulgur. You may need to stop and scrape down the sides a few times. Spread the cauliflower pieces on a large, clean kitchen towel to absorb excess liquid (parsnips will be drier, so skip this step if using them). Transfer the cauliflower or parsnip pieces to a large bowl. Add the garlic, cucumber, tomato, parsley, mint, lemon juice, and salt. Stir gently to combine all the vegetables, herbs, and seasonings.

MAKES 4 SERVINGS

Thai Sweet and Spicy Cucumber Salad

I got the inspiration for this salad from an Australian blogger named Thom. He combined cucumbers, sweet chili sauce, cilantro, and peanuts to make a lovely Thai salad. Thom's site is currently inactive, but I'm forever grateful to him for the idea behind this salad. For this recipe, I've created a version of sweet chili sauce that is free of refined sugar and preservatives. I think you'll enjoy it as much as the original.

- 2 large English cucumbers, cut into 1/2-inch dice
- 1/4 cup Date Paste (page 16)
- 1 tablespoon rice vinegar
- 1/2 teaspoon red pepper flakes
- 1 clove garlic, minced
- Sea salt and ground black pepper
- 1/4 cup minced cilantro
- 2 tablespoons crushed dry-roasted peanuts

Place the cucumbers in a large bowl and set aside.

In a small bowl, combine the Date Paste, vinegar, red pepper flakes, and garlic, and blend with a wire whisk until well combined. Pour the dressing over the cucumbers and toss to combine.

Divide the cucumbers and dressing among four salad plates. Season with salt and pepper, to taste. Top each salad with a sprinkling of the cilantro and the crushed peanuts.

MAKES 4 SERVINGS

Abe's Hearty Lentil Soup (page 126)

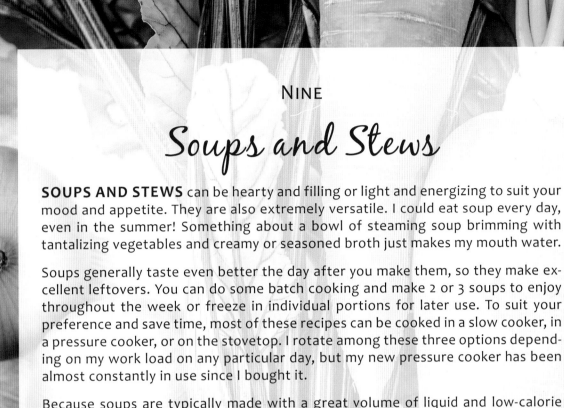

NINE

Soups and Stews

SOUPS AND STEWS can be hearty and filling or light and energizing to suit your mood and appetite. They are also extremely versatile. I could eat soup every day, even in the summer! Something about a bowl of steaming soup brimming with tantalizing vegetables and creamy or seasoned broth just makes my mouth water.

Soups generally taste even better the day after you make them, so they make excellent leftovers. You can do some batch cooking and make 2 or 3 soups to enjoy throughout the week or freeze in individual portions for later use. To suit your preference and save time, most of these recipes can be cooked in a slow cooker, in a pressure cooker, or on the stovetop. I rotate among these three options depending on my work load on any particular day, but my new pressure cooker has been almost constantly in use since I bought it.

Because soups are typically made with a great volume of liquid and low-calorie vegetables, they are both filling and hydrating without making you gain weight. The serving sizes in this chapter are big, typically between 2 and 3 cups of soup per person, so enjoy it and don't feel guilty if you want to go back for a second bowl.

Abe's Hearty Lentil Soup

My brother Abe was one of the biggest catalysts for my adopting a vegan diet. He taught me that a diet without animal foods can be incredibly delicious and abundant. He's been one of my closest friends and biggest supporters throughout the years. Abe has always had great rustic, down-home-style cooking skills. This is an adaptation of his famous lentil soup. It's hearty, filling, and comforting, just like lentil soup ought to be. You can visit Abe at his art print making site, AbrahamMcCowan.com.

6 cups vegetable broth

2 medium onions, cut into 1/4-inch dice (about 2 cups)

2 large ribs celery, cut into 1/4-inch dice

3 large carrots, cut into 1/2-inch slices

3 Roma tomatoes, cut into 1/2-inch dice

3 cloves garlic, minced

1 1/2 cups dry brown or green lentils, picked over and rinsed well

1 1/2 tablespoons nutritional yeast

1 1/2 tablespoons tamari or Bragg Liquid Aminos

3/4 teaspoon garlic powder

3/4 teaspoon dried dill

1/3 cup tomato paste

1/3 teaspoon ground cumin

1 teaspoon Spike or other herb seasoning (optional)

Salt and ground black pepper to taste

Heat 1/4 cup of the broth in a large soup pot over medium-high heat. Add the onions and sauté until tender and translucent, 3 to 5 minutes, adding additional broth as necessary. Add the celery, carrots, and tomatoes and cook until they begin to soften. Add the garlic and sauté for a minute or two more. Add the lentils, nutritional yeast, tamari, remaining vegetable broth, garlic powder, dill, tomato paste, cumin, and Spike, if using. Bring to a boil over medium-high heat. Cover the pot with a lid and reduce heat to a simmer. Cook for 45 to 60 minutes, or until the lentils are very tender.

Check the flavor and season to taste with salt and a few grinds of ground black pepper. The soup can be served as is or pulsed a few times with an immersion blender for a creamier finish.

MAKES 4 SERVINGS

Note: Many of my testers were concerned about adding the dill to this soup. Don't be afraid of it. It adds a subtle but delicious flavor that everyone was happy with once they tried it.

Cozy Roasted Butternut Soup

The first time I had butternut soup, I was living in Australia. That was the first time I'd eaten any orange squash in any dish that wasn't sweet or associated with pie. It was like a revelation, eating this mostly savory, slightly sweet vegetable soup. Where had it been all my life? All I know is that I haven't been able to stop making it since. (Also see photo on page 128.)

1 whole head garlic

1 large butternut squash, halved lengthwise, seeds left in

2 medium onions, halved lengthwise, skins removed and left intact

4 cups vegetable broth

1/4 cup dry sherry (optional)

1 1/2 teaspoons dried thyme

Dash of cayenne

1 1/2 tablespoons nutritional yeast

1/4 cup raw cashew pieces (optional)

1 teaspoon sea salt, or to taste

1/4 teaspoon ground black pepper

Preheat the oven to 425°F. Wrap the head of garlic in aluminum foil. Line a large rimmed baking sheet with parchment paper.

Arrange the squash halves cut side up on the prepared baking sheet, along with the onions cut-side down, and the foil-wrapped garlic. Roast the vegetables for 45 to 60 minutes or until everything is soft and lightly browned. About 20 minutes before the vegetables are finished, combine the vegetable broth, dry sherry (if using), thyme, cayenne, and nutritional yeast in a large soup pot over the lowest heat.

Once the vegetables are fully roasted, remove the baking tray from the oven and set aside until the vegetables are cool enough to handle. Now you can easily scoop out the butternut seeds with a large spoon or ice cream scoop and discard them or set them aside for toasting. Scoop the roasted butternut squash out of its shell. Roughly chop the roasted onions into 1-inch pieces. Cut the top quarter off the roasted garlic and squeeze out all the roasted cloves. Add the roasted squash, onions, and garlic to the simmering broth. Warm the soup over medium heat.

Once the vegetables are heated through, puree them completely with an immersion blender (or in batches through your regular blender). If using cashews, blend 1 cup of the hot pureed soup with the cashews in a blender until smooth, then return it to the pot and stir until combined.

MAKES 4 SERVINGS

Note: You can throw this soup together quickly on a weeknight if you use frozen or fresh pre-cut butternut squash. The onions, garlic, and squash can be chopped and sautéed in broth rather than roasted to cut off additional time. The result will still be delicious, but will have a little less depth than the original recipe.

Cheesy Smoky Spicy Black Bean Soup

My friend Donna, who is not vegan, says this is one of her favorite soups. Ever. I pretty much feel the same. I hope you will, too.

1 medium onion, coarsely chopped (1 cup)
3 Anaheim peppers, coarsely chopped
1 red bell pepper, coarsely chopped
3 cups vegetable broth
3 medium garlic cloves, minced
1 large carrot, cut into 1/4 inch slices
3 Roma tomatoes, cut into 1/4-inch dice, divided
2 (15.5-ounce) cans black beans, drained and rinsed
1 heaped tablespoon ground cumin
1 teaspoon dried oregano
1 1/2 teaspoons chili powder
1 teaspoon smoked paprika
1/8 teaspoon cayenne pepper
2 tablespoons tahini
2/3 cup nutritional yeast
1 teaspoon sea salt, or to taste
1/2 cup chopped fresh cilantro, for garnish
1/4 cup Cashew Sour Cream (page 154), optional garnish

Place the onions, Anaheim peppers, and red bell pepper on a large foil-lined baking sheet. Mist the vegetables with a quick burst of nonstick cooking spray. Set the oven to broil on high and broil the vegetables for 5 to 10 minutes until they are a little bit charred, watch carefully so they don't burn to a crisp.

Add the charred vegetables to a large saucepan. Add 1/4 cup of the vegetable broth over medium heat. Add the garlic, carrots, and 1/3 of the tomatoes and simmer until the onions soften, 2 to 3 minutes. Add the remaining vegetable broth, black beans, cumin, oregano, chili powder, smoked paprika, and cayenne. Reduce the heat to low, cover with a lid, and cook the soup for 20 minutes more.

Add the tahini, nutritional yeast, and salt to taste, stirring until smooth. Pulse the soup a few times with an immersion blender or pulse in batches in your blender. Top with the remaining diced tomato, chopped cilantro, and Cashew Sour Cream, if desired.

MAKES 4 SERVINGS

Chipotle Corn Chowder

Sweet corn, savory broth, and spicy chipotle are the perfect combination in this new take on the classic corn chowder.

3 cups vegetable broth

1 1/2 cups sweet onion, cut into 1/4-inch dice

2 large garlic cloves, minced

2 large carrots, cut into 1/4-inch slices

2 large ribs celery, cut into 1/4-inch dice

1 Roma tomato, cut into 1/4-inch dice

1 teaspoon coriander pods, crushed lightly with a mortar and pestle

1 teaspoon ground cumin

3 cups unsweetened almond milk

1 (16-ounce) bag organic frozen corn

1/4 teaspoon liquid smoke

1/2 cup raw cashew pieces (soaked for 4 to 6 hours)

3 tablespoons tapioca starch

1/4 to 1 teaspoon ground chipotle powder (start with the lesser amount and add more to taste)

1/2 cup roughly chopped fresh cilantro

1 teaspoon sea salt, or to taste

1/4 teaspoon ground black pepper

In a large soup pot, heat 1/4 cup of the vegetable broth over medium-high heat. Add the onion and sauté until nearly translucent, adding more broth as necessary. Add the garlic, carrots, celery, tomato, coriander, and cumin, and sauté for a few minutes more. Add the remaining vegetable broth, almond milk, corn, and liquid smoke. Put the lid on the pot and simmer for about 20 minutes.

Remove two cups of the soup and blend with the cashews and the tapioca starch until completely smooth and creamy. Return to the pot. Cook for 5 minutes, more then stir in the chipotle powder and the cilantro. Season with the salt and pepper. This soup can be pulsed a few times with an immersion blender for a creamier soup, if desired.

MAKES 4 SERVINGS

Cheesiest Potato Soup

One of the hardest things for people switching to a vegan diet is ditching the dairy. There's just something about creamy and cheesy foods that makes them hard to let go. This soup shows you that you can have your (vegan) creamy and cheesy flavors and not miss a thing! I've served this dish to multiple families who are not vegan, and they say they can't tell it isn't made with milk and cheese.

4 cups vegetable broth

1 medium onion, cut into 1/4-inch dice (about 1 cup)

1 large carrot, cut into 1/4-inch slices

1 large celery rib, cut into 1/4-inch slices

1 large clove garlic, minced

3 medium red potatoes (about 16 ounces), scrubbed or peeled, and cut into 1/2-inch dice

1 tablespoon dried or fresh parsley

1 cup water

1/2 cup raw cashew pieces (soaked for 4 to 6 hours)

1 tablespoon tomato paste

1 tablespoon fresh or bottled lemon juice

1/2 teaspoon smoked paprika

1 teaspoon ground mustard powder

1/4 teaspoon turmeric

1 tablespoon mellow white miso

1/4 cup nutritional yeast

Dash of cayenne

3 tablespoons tapioca starch or non-GMO cornstarch

1 teaspoon sea salt, or to taste

1/4 teaspoon ground black pepper

Heat 1/4 cup of the vegetable broth in a large soup pot over medium heat. Add the onion, carrot, and celery, and sauté until the onion is translucent, about 5 minutes. Add additional broth if necessary to keep the vegetables from burning. Add the garlic and sauté for a minute or two more. Add the remaining vegetable broth, potatoes, and parsley and bring to a boil. Reduce the heat to a simmer, cover, and cook for 15 to 20 minutes.

While the soup is simmering, in a high-speed blender, combine the water, cashews, tomato paste, lemon juice, smoked paprika, mustard powder, turmeric, miso, nutritional yeast, cayenne, and tapioca starch and blend until very smooth and creamy, 1 to 2 minutes.

Pour the blended liquid into the pot of soup and let simmer for a few minutes more. The cashew cream will thicken the soup a bit. Add the salt and pepper, to taste. For a thicker, creamier soup, put half the soup through the blender or pulse several times with an immersion blender.

MAKES 4 SERVINGS

Note: This recipe can easily be made into cheesy broccoli soup. Simply substitute 1 medium head of finely chopped broccoli for the potatoes.

Lightened-Up Laksa

When I lived in Australia, there was an amazing Malaysian restaurant on the corner of George Street in Sydney, right near where I worked. Whenever possible, I would go there for a huge, steaming bowl of laksa with the most delicious tofu and seasoned red pepper oil. My mouth waters and my heart aches just thinking about it. I've recreated a lighter, vegan version of laksa here that, while not quite as perfect as the original, will still send your taste buds sailing, perhaps to the island of Malaysia. If you're ever in Sydney, find that Malaysian restaurant!

14 ounces extra-firm tofu, drained, pressed, and cut into 1-inch dice

1 ounce thin bean thread noodles

1/4 cup dry roasted peanuts (soaked for 4 to 6 hours)

2 cups water

1 teaspoon to 1 tablespoon red curry paste (to taste)

1 (13.5-ounce) can light coconut milk

2 cups unsweetened coconut milk (from a carton)

2 cups vegetable broth

1 large carrot, cut into matchsticks

1/4 head green cabbage, torn into bite-sized pieces

3 to 4 large leaves bok choy, torn into bite-sized pieces

2 tablespoons fresh ginger, shaved with a vegetable peeler or grated

2 large cloves garlic, minced

Zest and juice of 1 large lime

1 tablespoon agave or pure maple syrup

2 tablespoons tamari or Bragg Liquid Aminos

1 teaspoon sea salt, or to taste

4 chopped scallions, for garnish

Fresh basil and mint leaves, for garnish

Sambal olek chili paste, for garnish

Preheat oven to 450°F. Place the cubed tofu on a baking sheet lined with a Silpat mat or parchment paper. Sprinkle with salt, if desired. Bake for 20 to 25 minutes until crispy, turning once. While the tofu is baking, soak the bean thread noodles in hot water until soft, 5 to 10 minutes. Drain and set aside. While the noodles are soaking, blend the peanuts, water, and red curry paste in a blender until completely smooth. Add the blended liquid to a large soup pot with the canned coconut milk, the carton coconut milk, and the vegetable broth. Heat over medium-high heat. Add the carrot, cabbage, bok choy, ginger, garlic, lime zest and juice, agave, and tamari. Reduce the heat and simmer for 10 minutes, until the vegetables are just crisp-tender. Remove the pot from the heat and season with salt to taste. Divide the bean thread noodles among 4 large soup bowls. Ladle the soup over the noodles and garnish with equal amounts of the baked tofu, scallions, basil, mint, and as much of the chili paste as desired.

MAKES 4 SERVINGS

Cream of Broccoli Soup

This traditional favorite soup has been deliciously retooled to remove heavy fats and cholesterol. It will leave you feeling full and satisfied, without that icky feeling you get after eating dairy-laden food.

- 4 cups vegetable broth
- 1 cup onion, cut into 1/4-inch dice
- 1 large rib celery, cut into 1/4-inch slices
- 1 medium clove garlic, minced
- 1 small head broccoli, cut into small florets (about 4 cups)
- 1 cup water
- 1/2 cup raw cashew pieces (soaked for 4 to 6 hours)
- 1 tablespoon lemon juice
- 1 tablespoon ground mustard powder
- 1 tablespoon mellow white miso
- 2 tablespoons nutritional yeast
- 3 tablespoons tapioca starch or non-GMO cornstarch
- 1 teaspoon sea salt, or to taste
- 1/4 teaspoon ground black pepper

Heat 1/4 cup of the vegetable broth in a large soup pot over medium-high heat. Add the onion and celery and sauté until the onion is translucent, about 5 minutes. Add additional broth to keep the vegetables from burning, if necessary. Add the garlic and sauté for 1 to 2 minutes longer. Add the remaining vegetable broth and broccoli and bring to a boil. Reduce the heat to a simmer, cover, and cook for 15 to 20 minutes.

While the soup is simmering, blend the water, cashews, lemon juice, mustard powder, miso, nutritional yeast, and tapioca starch in a blender until smooth and creamy, 1 to 2 minutes. Pour the cashew mixture into the soup and cook for a few minutes longer to thicken. Season with salt and pepper. For a smoother, creamier soup, put half of the soup through the blender or pulse several times with an immersion blender.

MAKES 4 SERVINGS

Cream of Mushroom Soup

I grew up being a huge fan of the mushroom soup that comes in a can. You know, the one that you have to shake to get the soup to squiggle its way out of the can like Jello, still retaining the marks from the inside of the can? Kind of gross if you think about it, but I loved it. However, this is better. I promise!

6 cups vegetable broth
1 medium onion, cut into 1/4-inch dice (1 cup)
3 medium cloves garlic, minced
1 pound mushrooms, cut into 1/4-inch thick slices
1/4 cup dry sherry (optional)
1/2 teaspoon dried oregano
1/2 teaspoon dried thyme
1/2 cup raw cashews (soaked for 4 to 6 hours)
2 tablespoons nutritional yeast
1 teaspoon sea salt, or to taste
1/4 teaspoon ground black pepper

Heat 1/4 cup of the vegetable broth in a large soup pot over medium-high heat. Add the onion and sauté until the onion softens and becomes translucent, 3 to 5 minutes. Add the garlic and sauté 1 to 2 minutes longer, adding more vegetable broth as needed to keep the onion and garlic from burning. Add the mushrooms to the pot and sauté until they have softened and released their liquid, 3 to 5 minutes. Add the remaining vegetable broth, sherry, oregano, and thyme. Reduce the heat to medium-low and simmer for 20 minutes.

Transfer 2 cups of the hot soup to a blender. Add the cashews and nutritional yeast and blend until completely creamy, 1 to 2 minutes. Return the liquid to the pot and season with salt and pepper. Heat the soup for 5 more minutes or until slightly thickened.

MAKES 4 SERVINGS

Creamy White Bean, Potato, and Kale Soup with Mushroom "Sausage"

This spicy and comforting soup mimics one from a famous Italian restaurant chain. This lightened up vegan version uses mushrooms for a natural "sausage" and cashews for creaminess. This version is as delicious as the restaurant version without the dairy cream and pork sausage.

4 cups vegetable broth

8 ounces button mushrooms, cut into ¼-inch dice

1 1/2 teaspoons fennel seeds, crushed lightly between your fingers

1/4 to 1 teaspoon red pepper flakes, to taste

1 teaspoon Italian seasoning

1 teaspoon liquid smoke

1 cup chopped onion

2 ribs celery, cut into 1/4-inch dice

1 medium carrot, cut into 1/4-inch dice

2 large cloves garlic, minced

2 to 3 Yukon gold potatoes (about 1 pound), scrubbed, skins left on, cut into 1-inch dice

1/4 cup dry sherry

1 (15.5-ounce) can cannellini or other white beans, drained and rinsed

1/2 cup cashews (soaked for 4 to 6 hours)

1 cup water

2 tablespoons nutritional yeast

4 cups dinosaur or lacinato kale, cut into thin 1/4-inch ribbons

1 teaspoon sea salt, or to taste

1/4 teaspoon ground black pepper

Heat 1/4 cup of the vegetable broth in a large soup pot over medium-high heat. Add the mushrooms and cook until they release their juices and cook down in size, about 5 minutes. Add the fennel seeds, red pepper flakes, Italian seasoning, and liquid smoke and stir to combine.

Add the onion and sauté until translucent, 3 to 5 minutes, adding more broth as needed. Add celery and carrot and sauté for a few minutes more. Add the garlic and potatoes and sauté 1 minute longer. Add the remaining vegetable broth, sherry, and white beans. Cover the pot with a lid and reduce heat to a simmer. Cook for 20 to 25 minutes, or until the potatoes are fork-tender.

In a blender, combine the cashew pieces, water, and nutritional yeast, and blend until completely smooth and creamy, 1 to 2 minutes. Add the cashew cream to the pot, then add the kale ribbons and season with the salt and pepper. This soup will thicken slightly upon standing and become even thicker with refrigeration.

MAKES 4 SERVINGS

Lightened-Up African Peanut Stew

My friend Amanda, who runs the site GoodCleanFood, makes the best African peanut stew. This is a lighter adaptation of her version. I love simmering this recipe in a slow cooker all day in cold weather. It is just delightful and comforting.

4 cups vegetable broth

1 large onion, cut into 1/4-inch dice (about 2 cups)

2 large carrots, cut into 1/4-inch thin slices

1 small red bell pepper, cut into 1/2-inch dice

2 to 3 large cloves garlic, pressed or minced

1 tablespoon grated fresh ginger

1 tablespoon agave or pure maple syrup

1 teaspoon ground cumin

1 teaspoon ground cinnamon

1/4 teaspoon cayenne pepper

1/4 cup PB2 or other defatted peanut flour

1 (12-ounce) sweet potato, peeled and cut into 1/2-inch cubes

1 (15.5-ounce) can red kidney beans, drained and rinsed

1 (14.5-ounce) can diced tomatoes, undrained

1/2 to 1 bunch dinosaur or lacinato kale, ribs removed and cut into 1/4-inch ribbons

1 teaspoon sea salt, or to taste

1/4 teaspoon ground black pepper

2 tablespoons finely chopped roasted peanuts (for garnish)

1/2 cup roughly chopped cilantro (for garnish)

Heat 1/4 cup of the vegetable broth in a large soup pot over medium-high heat. Add the onion and carrots and sauté until the onion begins to soften, about 5 minutes. Add more broth as necessary to keep the vegetables from burning. Add the bell pepper, cover loosely, and cook a few more minutes. Add the garlic and ginger, and sauté, stirring, for 1 to 2 minutes, then add the agave, cumin, cinnamon, and cayenne. Cook for 1 minute to allow the flavors to bloom. Stir in the PB2 or peanut flour until evenly distributed, then add the sweet potatoes, kidney beans, diced tomatoes, and the remaining vegetable broth.

Bring the soup to a boil, then cover and simmer until sweet potatoes are very soft, 25 to 30 minutes. Stir in the kale during the last few minutes of cooking, to soften just slightly. Add the salt and black pepper. Divide into four large bowls and garnish with the chopped peanuts and cilantro.

MAKES 4 SERVINGS

Tomato Basil Bisque

This bisque will remind you of dining at your favorite bistro. This vegan version tastes just like the dairy version, if not better.

- 3 cups vegetable broth
- 1 cup red onion, cut into 1/4-inch dice
- 3 large garlic cloves, minced
- 1 (28-ounce) can crushed tomatoes
- 1 teaspoon Italian seasoning
- 2 tablespoons dry sherry (optional)
- 1 teaspoon agave or pure maple syrup
- 1 tablespoon tamari or Bragg Liquid Aminos
- 1/2 cup raw cashew pieces (soaked for 4 to 6 hours)
- 1 cup water
- 1/4 cup packed roughly chopped fresh basil
- 1 teaspoon sea salt, or to taste
- 1/4 teaspoon ground black pepper

Heat 1/4 cup of the vegetable broth in a large soup pot over medium-high heat. Add the onion and sauté, stirring occasionally, for about 5 minutes, or until the onion is softened. Add additional broth as necessary to keep it from burning. Add the garlic and sauté for 1 to 2 minutes, adding more broth as necessary. Add the tomatoes, remaining vegetable broth, sherry (if using), Italian seasoning, agave, and tamari. Cover the soup with a lid and reduce heat to a simmer.

While the soup is simmering, blend the cashew pieces with the water until completely smooth and creamy, 1 to 2 minutes. Pour the liquid into the soup pot and stir to combine. Add the basil and season with the salt and black pepper.

MAKES 4 SERVINGS

Note: For a completely creamy soup, blend it with an immersion blender or in batches in your blender. One of my testers, Poppy from the blog The Bunny Kitchen, added a roasted red pepper to this soup. If you have an extra roasted red pepper on hand, it's a fabulous addition.

Moroccan Lentil Soup

My Australian sister-in-law Annette made this soup for us while her family was here vacationing in the United States. At the time, she couldn't find "Moroccan spice" at the local grocery store, something I assume is easily available in Australia. She improvised, using some curry powders in my cupboard, for delicious but not-quite-right results. I was intrigued by the soup and wanted to make it again with the right seasonings, so I did some research on what "Moroccan spice" might be. Here's my interpretation of this soup, which is easily the most popular soup recipe on my website.

6 cups vegetable broth

2 cups chopped onion, cut into 1/4-inch dice

2 medium carrots, sliced into 1/4-inch rounds

2 large cloves garlic, minced or pressed

1 teaspoon ground coriander

1 1/2 heaped teaspoons ground cumin

3/4 teaspoon ground turmeric

3/4 teaspoon smoked paprika

3/4 teaspoon ground cinnamon

3/4 teaspoon ground ginger

1 (28-ounce) can crushed tomatoes

1 1/2 cups split dry red lentils, picked over and rinsed

1/3 cup chopped parsley

1/3 cup chopped cilantro

Juice of 1 large lemon

1 teaspoon sea salt, or to taste

1/3 teaspoon ground black pepper

Heat 1/4 cup of the vegetable broth in a large soup pot over medium-high heat. Add the onion, carrot, and garlic and sauté, adding additional broth as necessary to keep the vegetables from burning. Sauté until the onions are softened and translucent, about 5 minutes. Add the coriander, cumin, turmeric, smoked paprika, cinnamon, and ground ginger. Sauté the vegetables and seasonings for 1 to 2 minutes to allow the flavors to bloom. Add the remaining vegetable broth, crushed tomatoes, and lentils and bring to a boil.

Cover the pot and reduce the heat to a simmer. Cook for 30 minutes or until the lentils are fully cooked. Add the parsley, cilantro, and lemon juice and stir to combine. Season with the salt and pepper. For texture variation you can pulse the soup a few times with an immersion blender. For extra brightness, squeeze an additional slice of lemon over each bowl.

MAKES 4 SERVINGS

Quinoa Minestrone

This minestrone uses non-traditional quinoa instead of pasta. Because this soup is largely flavored by its vegetable broth, I suggest using a good one such as Better Than Bouillon Vegan Chicken Base or Edward and Sons Vegan Chicken Broth Cubes. This soup is brimming with delicious vegetables. If you prefer other vegetables in your minestrone, simply substitute your favorites.

- 6 cups vegetable broth
- 1 1/4 cups chopped onion, cut into 1/4-inch dice
- 4 large carrots, cut into 1/4-inch slices
- 3 medium cloves garlic, minced
- 1 (15.5-ounce) can kidney beans, drained and rinsed
- 1 teaspoon dried thyme
- 1 (14.5-ounce) can petite diced tomatoes, undrained
- 1 cup fresh or frozen green beans, ends trimmed, cut into 1-inch pieces
- 1/3 cup quinoa, well rinsed
- 2 tablespoons tamari or Bragg Liquid Aminos
- 2 tablespoons nutritional yeast
- 1 teaspoon sea salt, or to taste
- 1/4 teaspoon ground black pepper
- 2 cups packed fresh baby spinach, cut into 1/4-inch ribbons
- 1/4 cup roughly chopped fresh basil

Heat 1/4 cup of the vegetable broth in a large soup pot over medium-high heat. Add the onion and carrot and sauté for 5 minutes, adding additional broth as necessary to keep the vegetables from burning. Once the onion is translucent, add the garlic and sauté 1 to 2 minutes. Add the remaining vegetable broth, kidney beans, thyme, tomatoes, green beans, quinoa, tamari, and nutritional yeast.

Bring the soup to a low boil. Cover with a lid and reduce the heat to medium-low. Simmer for 25 to 30 minutes, or until the quinoa and vegetables are cooked through. Season with the salt and pepper. Add the spinach and simmer 1 to 2 minutes longer, then sprinkle with the fresh basil and serve immediately.

MAKES 4 SERVINGS

Smoky Split Pea Soup

I grew up eating split pea soup cooked with a ham bone. This soup is ham bone-free, but it tastes like it was cooked just like the original. If you think you're not a fan of split pea soup, give this a try. You may be surprised by you how much you love it.

- **5 cups vegetable broth**
- **1 cup chopped onion**
- **4 medium carrots, cut into 1/4-inch slices**
- **2 large ribs celery, cut into 1/4-inch slices**
- **2 medium cloves garlic, minced or pressed**
- **1 teaspoon dried thyme**
- **1 teaspoon dried oregano**
- **1 teaspoon to 1 tablespoon liquid smoke (use the lesser amount if you have a concentrated brand such as Wrights)**
- **1 1/2 cups dried split peas**
- **2 bay leaves**
- **Dash of cayenne**
- **1 teaspoon sea salt, or to taste**
- **1/4 teaspoon ground black pepper**

Heat 1/4 cup of the vegetable broth in a large soup pot over medium-high heat. Add the onion, carrots, celery, garlic, thyme, and oregano and sauté until the onion is translucent. Add additional vegetable broth as needed to keep the vegetables from burning. Add the remaining vegetable broth, liquid smoke, split peas, bay leaves, and cayenne, and bring to a boil.

Reduce the heat to low and simmer with the lid on for 45 to 60 minutes, or until the split peas are very tender. Remove the bay leaves and season with the salt and pepper. Serve as is, or blend until smooth, or pulse a few times with an immersion blender (my favorite method) for a slightly thickened but still chunky soup.

MAKES 4 SERVINGS

Vegan Pho

This Vietnamese soup is inspired by the vegan pho at Oh Mai, one of my favorite restaurants in Salt Lake City. They have multiple vegan selections on the menu and the prices are (borderline ridiculously) cheap. But the best part is that their food is simply fantastic. The portion size for this soup really is 4 servings—it is one huge bowl of soup—so if you have those lovely large Asian bowls, now is the time to use them!

BROTH
1 teaspoon toasted sesame oil
1 cup roughly chopped yellow onion
6 large cloves garlic, sliced
12 cups vegetable broth
1/4 cup tamari or Bragg Liquid Aminos
2 tablespoons fresh ginger, shaved into pieces with a vegetable peeler
1 teaspoon ground black pepper
4 whole star anise
1 teaspoon sea salt, or to taste
2 large carrots, cut into 1/8-inch rounds

NOODLES AND VEGETABLES
2 ounces thin rice noodles or bean thread
2 small heads baby bok choy, cut lengthwise into eighths
4 to 6 iceberg lettuce leaves, roughly torn into bite-sized pieces
14 ounces extra-firm tofu, drained, pressed, and cut into 1/4-inch rectangular pieces
1 cup loosely packed Thai basil (or whatever basil you can find)
1/2 cup loosely packed fresh torn mint leaves
4 scallions, cut into 1/4 inch pieces
1 small red onion, quartered and cut into thin slivers (about 3/4 cup)
1/4 cup lightly packed chopped cilantro
2 medium jalapeños, cut into thin rounds
4 cups fresh bean sprouts
2 limes, quartered
Sriracha sauce, for serving

Heat the sesame oil in a large stock pot over medium-high heat. Once the oil is shimmering, add the onion and cook, stirring, until nearly translucent, adding splashes of the vegetable broth as necessary. Add the garlic and sauté for 1 to 2 minutes, then stir in the vegetable broth, tamari, ginger, black pepper, and star anise and bring to a boil. Cover, reduce the heat to medium-low, and simmer for 15 minutes. Strain the broth to remove the garlic, onion, ginger, and star anise. Discard the vegetables and spices. Taste the broth and season with salt to taste, if needed. Add the carrots to the broth and keep warm over low heat. While the broth is simmering, prep your other ingredients.

Soak the noodles in hot water for 5 to 10 minutes, then drain and set aside.

To the simmering broth, add the bok choy, lettuce, and tofu. Simmer on low for a few minutes while you arrange the bowls. Divide the noodles among the 4 bowls and swirl them into a circle at the bottom of the bowl. Cover the noodles with the steaming broth and vegetables (about 3 cups broth per bowl). Garnish each bowl with the basil, mint, scallions, red onion, cilantro, jalapeño, bean sprouts, squeezes of fresh lime juice, and sriracha, as desired.

MAKES 4 SERVINGS

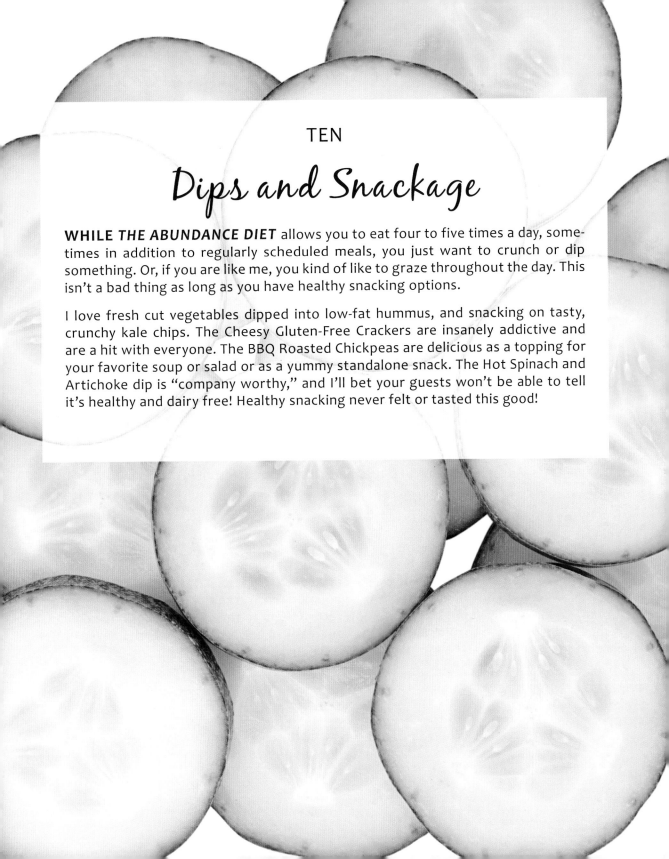

TEN

Dips and Snackage

WHILE *THE ABUNDANCE DIET* allows you to eat four to five times a day, some-times in addition to regularly scheduled meals, you just want to crunch or dip something. Or, if you are like me, you kind of like to graze throughout the day. This isn't a bad thing as long as you have healthy snacking options.

I love fresh cut vegetables dipped into low-fat hummus, and snacking on tasty, crunchy kale chips. The Cheesy Gluten-Free Crackers are insanely addictive and are a hit with everyone. The BBQ Roasted Chickpeas are delicious as a topping for your favorite soup or salad or as a yummy standalone snack. The Hot Spinach and Artichoke dip is "company worthy," and I'll bet your guests won't be able to tell it's healthy and dairy free! Healthy snacking never felt or tasted this good!

Baked Nacho Cheesy Kale Chips

I'm telling the truth when I say that you might be able to plow through these super-tasty kale chips faster than through a bag of Nacho Cheese Doritos. Thankfully, this is one indulgent snack that you don't have to feel guilty about! If you feel hesitant because you've never made kale chips, let go of your inhibitions and give these a try. Even my kale-hating husband can't get enough of these fantastic chips.

1 medium red bell pepper, cut into 1-inch pieces

1 medium clove garlic, minced

1/4 cup cashew pieces, soaked for 4 to 6 hours

2 tablespoons mellow white miso

1/4 cup nutritional yeast

1 tablespoon tamari or Bragg Liquid Aminos

2 tablespoons lime juice

1 tablespoon chili powder

1 teaspoon ground cumin

Dash of cayenne

1/2 teaspoon sea salt (or to taste)

1/4 teaspoon ground black pepper

1 (10-ounce) bunch dinosaur or lacinato kale, washed, dried, and torn into 2 to 3-inch pieces

Preheat your oven to its very lowest heat setting (mine is 170°F). In a blender or food processor, combine the red bell pepper, garlic, cashews, miso, nutritional yeast, tamari, lime juice, chili powder, cumin, and cayenne. Blend the ingredients until smooth and creamy, 1 to 2 minutes. Add the salt and black pepper. This is your awesome nacho sauce.

Add the kale to a large salad bowl and pour the nacho sauce over it. Toss the kale leaves with the nacho sauce until the leaves are completely coated.

Lightly spray 2 rimmed large baking sheets with cooking spray. Divide the kale leaves evenly between the two baking sheets. Bake for 1 hour, then remove the baking sheets from the oven and turn the kale leaves over using a thin spatula. Rotate the baking sheets in the oven top to bottom, then bake for 1 hour longer. The kale chips should be crisp and ready to eat at this point. If they are not, return them to the oven and continue baking, checking every 20 to 30 minutes until they are ready to eat. Kale chips will crisp even more upon cooling. They can be stored in an airtight container at room temperature for up to one week.

MAKES 4 SERVINGS

Notes: If you adore kale, you can use two heads of kale for this recipe, or about 20 ounces. The sauce won't be as pronounced, but you get to eat lots more kale for about the same amount of calories!

To make these in a dehydrator, use nonstick dehydrator sheets and dry on a low heat setting for 8 to 9 hours or until crisp, turning halfway through the drying time.

BBQ Roasted Chickpea Snack

I was tooling around in the kitchen making versions of chickpea bacon, but multiple people told me these taste like BBQ chickpeas instead of bacon. No loss, eh? These are absolutely fantastic for snacking on. You may want to make a double batch, as these are super addictive! They make a great salad topping and can be used instead of tofu in the Niçoise Salad (page 116).

1 tablespoon liquid smoke

1/2 teaspoon toasted sesame oil

3/4 teaspoon ground black pepper

1/2 teaspoon smoked paprika

1/2 teaspoon nutritional yeast

1/2 tablespoons pure maple syrup

1 1/2 teaspoons dry sherry

1 tablespoon tamari or Bragg Liquid Aminos

1/4 teaspoon onion powder

1/8 teaspoon garlic powder

1 (15.5-ounce) can chickpeas, drained, well rinsed and then blotted dry with a clean kitchen towel

Preheat the oven to 450°F. In a medium bowl, stir together the liquid smoke, sesame oil, black pepper, smoked paprika, nutritional yeast, maple syrup, sherry, tamari, onion powder, and garlic powder. This is your marinade. Add the chickpeas to the marinade and stir to coat.

Transfer the chickpeas and marinade into an 8x8-inch baking dish lined with parchment paper. Bake the chickpeas for 15 to 20 minutes, stirring once or twice. The chickpeas will get crispier as they cool. Store in a lidded container in the refrigerator. These are even better, if possible, on the second day.

MAKES 4 SERVINGS

Variations

Wasabi Chickpeas: Omit the liquid smoke and the smoked paprika in the marinade. Add 1/2 to 1 full teaspoon of dairy-free wasabi paste to the remaining ingredients and proceed with the recipe as directed. Wasabi Chickpeas are used in the Asian Cabbage Salad (page 98).

BBQ Tofu: This marinade is also great for making BBQ Tofu! Simply press a 14-ounce block of extra-firm tofu for 30 minutes, cut into 1/2-inch dice, and then follow the instructions for baking the chickpeas.

Cashew Sour Cream

When I first went vegan, I had already developed a love for soy and almond milks, but dairy sour cream was one of the dairy products I missed the most. Replacements in most cookbooks I had at the time simply called for tofu with some seasonings. These recipes tasted just like seasoned tofu to me, and not in a good way. Store-bought versions were better, but they were higher in fat and they contained some ingredients that I didn't like. They also lacked the delicious tang that I love in dairy sour cream. This recipe adds cashews to the traditional vegan recipe made just with tofu. The addition makes a creamier and more delicious vegan sour cream. The addition of vegan probiotic powder, if you can find it, adds just the right amount of tang to make mouths happy while making it very good for the gut too. Use this recipe anywhere you would normally use sour cream.

- 1 (12.3-ounce) box Mori Nu (or other brand) extra-firm silken tofu, drained and blotted dry
- 1/2 cup raw cashew pieces, soaked for 4 to 6 hours
- 2 tablespoons fresh or bottled lemon juice
- 1 teaspoon mellow white miso
- 1/2 teaspoon ground mustard powder
- 1/4 teaspoon or 1 to 2 capsules vegan probiotic powder
- 1/2 teaspoon sea salt, or to taste

Combine the tofu, cashews, lemon juice, miso, and mustard powder in a high-speed blender or a food processor. Blend until completely smooth. Add the probiotic powder and salt and blend until fully combined.

Cashew Sour Cream is a component to lots of the recipes in this book, so it's good to have some on hand in the refrigerator. It keeps well for at least 7 to 10 days stored in a lidded container.

MAKES ABOUT 2 CUPS (16 1-TABLESPOON SERVINGS)

Notes: A high-speed blender is the best equipment for making this recipe. If you don't have one, a food processor is the next best option, but you might not be able to get the cashews completely smooth so, if using a food processor, for a smoother finish you can try 1/4 cup raw cashew butter or 1/4 cup tahini instead of the raw cashews. The flavor will vary slightly from the original recipe, but using the nut or seed butter will give you a very nice and smooth finish.

Fire-Roasted Salsa

I'm not a huge fan of store-bought salsa, but I have always adored fresh homemade salsa even though I don't adore spending ages chopping tomatoes, onions and jalapeños. If you've ever made salsa, you know just how time-consuming it can be. Using a blender or food processor speeds things up, but it creates undesirable foam in salsas with the fresh ingredients I like to use. Here, I've come up with a fabulous compromise. A recipe that tastes as fresh as using garden tomatoes and jalapeños, but using canned tomatoes and chilies instead. This recipe takes less than two minutes to make, including the time it takes to open the cans, so you can have homemade salsa that tastes absolutely yummy in no time flat. I've won multiple church salsa contests with variations of this recipe, which is no small feat, as Mormons are super serious about canning and salsa.

1 (14.5-ounce) can fire-roasted diced tomatoes, undrained
1 medium clove garlic, minced
1 (4-ounce) can fire-roasted diced green chilies (mild, medium, or hot)
1/4 cup chopped red onion
2 tablespoons lemon or lime juice
1 teaspoon sriracha or your favorite hot sauce (omit if you prefer mild salsa)
1/2 cup roughly chopped cilantro
1 teaspoon sea salt, or to taste
1/4 teaspoon ground black pepper

In a blender or food processor, combine the tomatoes, garlic, green chilies, onion, lemon juice, sriracha if using, and cilantro. Pulse the ingredients 3 to 4 times in short bursts until everything is roughly chopped and combined.

Add the salt and pepper and pulse two more times to combine. This can be eaten immediately, but tastes even better after being refrigerated for 30 to 60 minutes. It will keep well in the refrigerator for up to one week in a sealed container.

MAKES 8 SERVINGS

Notes: If you can't find fire-roasted tomatoes and fire-roasted green chilies, use plain diced tomatoes and green chilies. The recipe will still be delicious!

For additional smoky flavor, add a couple drops of liquid smoke or use smoked salt in place of the sea salt.

Cheesy Gluten-Free Crackers

This recipe is a healthy version of those bright orange cheese crackers that are insanely addictive. These crackers aren't bright orange or full of weird ingredients and chemicals, but I think they're equally crunch-worthy. They are also a star component of my Vegan Egg Salad (page 114).

3/4 cup Somer's All-Purpose Gluten-Free Flour Blend (page 14)
1/4 cup nutritional yeast
1 1/2 teaspoons ground golden flaxseed
1/4 teaspoon smoked paprika
Scant 1/2 teaspoon sea salt (or to taste)
1/2 teaspoon garlic powder
1/8 teaspoon turmeric
Scant dash of cayenne
1 teaspoon lemon juice
1 tablespoon tahini (or almond butter)
4 tablespoons ice water, or more as needed

Preheat the oven to 350°F. In a medium bowl, combine the flour, nutritional yeast, ground flaxseed, smoked paprika, salt, garlic powder, turmeric, and cayenne. Mix well with a wire whisk. Add the lemon juice and tahini, cutting the tahini into the dry ingredients with a pastry cutter or fork until the dough is fine and crumbly. Add the water a tablespoon at a time until the dough becomes cohesive. You may need a little more or a little less than 5 tablespoons.

Transfer the dough onto a Silpat mat or piece of parchment paper large enough for your rimmed baking sheet. Roll out the dough, using a little extra flour if needed to keep it from sticking to your rolling pin. The dough should be fairly thin and nearly cover the whole Silpat or parchment paper. Cut the rolled dough into 1-inch squares. I like to use a crinkle cutter and dot the centers with the point of a chopstick to make them look like those famous cheese crackers.

Place the Silpat or parchment onto your baking sheet and bake for 15 minutes or until slightly golden and crisp. Remove the crackers from the oven and carefully pull the Silpat or parchment paper out from under them, leaving them behind on the tray. Bake the crackers for an additional 2 to 4 minutes more until they're nice and crisp. This recipe makes about 100 crackers and stores well in a sealed container for up to a week in the pantry.

MAKES 4 SERVINGS

Cucumber Tzatziki

This cool and creamy dip is the perfect complement to my falafel salad (page 104) but is also a delicious dip for your favorite fresh sliced vegetables.

- 1 medium cucumber, peeled (optional), seeded and cut into 1/4-inch dice
- 1/2 teaspoon sea salt, plus more if needed
- 1 cup Cashew Sour Cream (page 154)
- 1 small clove garlic, minced
- 1 tablespoon finely chopped fresh dill or 1 teaspoon dried dill
- 2 tablespoons finely minced fresh mint
- 1 teaspoon lemon juice

In a colander, toss together the cucumber and the salt, place in the sink and let drain for 20 to 30 minutes. Press the cucumbers with a clean, lint-free kitchen towel to absorb any excess moisture. Transfer the drained and pressed cucumbers to a medium-sized bowl. Add the cashew sour cream, garlic, dill, mint, and lemon juice. Stir to combine and add additional salt to taste if desired. For the best flavor, chill for one hour in the refrigerator before using to allow flavors to develop.

MAKES 4 SERVINGS

Hot Spinach and Artichoke Dip

Traditional spinach and artichoke dip is a huge calorie bomb! It typically contains full-fat dairy sour cream, butter, mayonnaise, mozzarella cheese and Parmesan cheese in addition to the vegetables the dish is named after. In this version, I make the vegetables the star of the show and replace the calorie-laden ingredients with my Cashew Sour Cream and my Fresh Vegan Moxarella. This dip is so rich and satisfying! You won't believe how healthy it is.

1/2 cup Cashew Sour Cream (page 154)
1 cup canned or freshly cooked navy beans, drained and rinsed
1 tablespoon nutritional yeast
1 tablespoon lemon juice
1 tablespoon tamari or Bragg Liquid Aminos
1 tablespoon dried onion flakes
Dash of cayenne
1/2 recipe Fresh Vegan Moxarella (page 16), divided
1 (14-ounce) can artichoke hearts packed in brine or water (not oil)
1/2 (10-ounce) package frozen spinach, thawed, drained, and water squeezed out
1 teaspoon sea salt
1/2 teaspoon ground black pepper
4 to 6 cups fresh or steamed cut vegetables (I like a combination of broccoli, carrots, cauliflower, and celery, but you can use your favorite vegetables)

Preheat the oven to 425°F. In a food processor, combine the cashew sour cream, navy beans, nutritional yeast, lemon juice, tamari, onion flakes, cayenne, and half of the Moxarella (about 1/4 cup). Process until completely smooth.

Add the artichoke hearts and the spinach to the food processor and pulse until the pieces are slightly broken down, but small chunks still remain. Add the salt and black pepper. Use a flexible spatula to scoop the dip out of the food processor and transfer into an oiled 8x8-inch glass or ceramic bakeware dish. Dot the remaining Moxarella (about 1/4 cup) over the top of the dip.

Bake the dip for 15 to 20 minutes or until heated through. If desired, broil the top for a few minutes more to let the Moxarella brown. Remove the dip from the oven and serve with the fresh or steamed vegetables.

MAKES 4 SERVINGS

Oil-Free Hummus

Plant-based guru Dreena Burton often says that hummus should be its own food group. I couldn't agree more! There are so many delicious ways to make hummus and so many things to do with it. It's one of the foods I almost always have in my fridge for a snack attack. I love to spread hummus on sandwiches and wraps. I also love to dip my favorite fresh vegetables in it. I even love a giant dollop of it on a salad instead of salad dressing. Most hummus is loaded with olive oil and tahini. Both are super yummy, but they make hummus a very calorie-dense food. This hummus is really light and healthy, but it tastes just as good as the varieties that are heavy on fat and calories. This is my basic recipe to get you dipping; multiple variations follow in the notes. In no time, you'll be coming up with your own favorite combinations. Eat as many fresh cut vegetables with this hummus as you wish, for a snack. I like it with cucumbers, tomatoes, carrots, celery, cauliflower, broccoli, and more.

> 1 (15.5-ounce) can garbanzo beans, drained and rinsed
> 2 tablespoons fresh or bottled lemon juice
> 1 clove garlic, minced
> 1/2 teaspoon ground cumin
> 1/2 teaspoon smoked paprika
> 1/4 to 1/3 cup of water (use just enough to process)
> 1/2 teaspoon sea salt, or to taste

In a blender or food processor, combine the garbanzo beans, lemon juice, garlic, cumin, smoked paprika, and 1/4 cup of water. Process until very smooth and creamy. Add additional water one tablespoon at a time if necessary. Add the salt and blend until distributed.

MAKES 4 SERVINGS

Hummus Variations

- **Avocado hummus:** add 1/2 of a small peeled, pitted and diced avocado to the hummus. (This recipe spoils more quickly and should be used on the day it is made).
- **Creamier hummus:** add 1 tablespoon of tahini.
- **Green chile hummus:** add 1 (4-ounce) can plain or fire-roasted green chiles.
- **Indian spiced hummus:** add 1 teaspoon each, ground coriander, black onion seeds, and black mustard seeds.
- **Olive hummus:** add 1/4 cup of your favorite variety of pitted olives.
- **Other bean hummus:** use black beans, pinto beans, navy beans, or your favorite bean instead of the chickpeas.
- **Roasted garlic hummus:** add 1 whole head of peeled and roasted garlic to the recipe.
- **Roasted red pepper hummus:** add one medium-sized roasted red pepper to the recipe.
- **Sriracha hummus:** add 1 tablespoon of sriracha to the recipe.
- **Spicy peanut butter hummus:** add 1 tablespoon of peanut butter and 1 teaspoon of your favorite hot sauce; use lime juice instead of lemon juice.
- **Sun-dried tomato hummus:** add 2 tablespoons of finely chopped dry pack sun-dried tomatoes. Omit the cumin and add one teaspoon of Italian seasonings.

Cheesy Herb and Vegetable Crust Pizza (page 168)

ELEVEN

Main Dishes

WHEN I ORIGINALLY DEVELOPED the challenge that became *The Abundance Diet,* it consisted mostly of smoothies, soups, and salads. While that was enough to keep most of the participants full, some of my blog readers were asking for heartier main courses. I've come up with some personal and family favorite recipes that are filling and scrumptious while keeping with the integrity of the diet. I still want you to have a soup, a salad, and a smoothie every day, too, but enjoy these delicious main courses for dinner. These meals can be served with any of the side salads in Chapter Eight, or paired with your favorite steamed or sautéed vegetables to round out your meal.

BBQ Tofu and Avocado Spring Rolls

I adore spring rolls! They are filled with such vibrant flavors. This version is a little East vs. West as the BBQ tofu pairs with the spicy peanut dipping sauce. This dish is best prepared with a helper who can soften the rice paper wrappers for you while you work with the vegetables and the rolling. You can certainly make these on your own, but it will be a little more time-consuming. Why not make it a family affair and have everyone roll their own using individual plates full of warm water?

Note: Soft lettuce such as red leaf, green leaf, or butter lettuce work best here. You'll need 16 leaves, or if you are using a big head of lettuce, you can tear the lettuce leaves in half.

16 rice paper wrappers (made with brown rice, if possible)

1 medium head lettuce (see Note above)

1 batch BBQ Tofu (page 152)

4 medium carrots, cut into 4-inch matchsticks or shaved with a vegetable peeler into fine ribbons

1 medium cucumber, cut into 4-inch matchsticks

1/2 cup lightly packed basil leaves, chopped

1/2 cup lightly packed mint leaves, chopped

1/4 small head of cabbage (green or purple) thinly sliced

1 small avocado, divided in half, pitted, and cut lengthwise into 8 thin strips on each side

Rice vinegar, for drizzling over vegetables

Sweet and Spicy Peanut Dipping Sauce (recipe follows)

Fill a shallow dinner plate with hot water, then dampen a clean, lint-free kitchen towel and ring out most of the water. This is your work surface. Submerge one rice paper wrapper at a time for about 30 seconds or until soft. Remove the wrapper from the water and place it on the towel. Arrange the lettuce in the center of the wrap (folding it if you need it to fit better) and arrange some of the BBQ tofu, carrots, cucumber, bail, mint, red cabbage, and avocado on top of the lettuce. Sprinkle the vegetables with about a half teaspoon of rice vinegar. Then, roll the wrap up like a burrito: fold the sides in over the toppings, then roll from the side facing you down to the end, sealing the vegetables in with the rice paper at the end.

Set the spring rolls aside on a clean plate as you make them. Don't let them touch, or they'll stick together! Repeat until all the fillings and rice paper wrappers are used. Serve with the dipping sauce.

MAKES 4 SERVINGS (16 ROLLS)

Sweet and Spicy Peanut Dipping Sauce

4 tablespoons PB2 or defatted peanut flour

2 tablespoons tamari or Bragg Liquid Aminos

4 tablespoons Date Paste (page 16)

Juice of 1 medium lime

1 medium clove garlic, very finely minced

1 teaspoon finely minced fresh ginger

1 teaspoon sriracha

2 to 4 tablespoons warm water

In a small bowl, whisk together the PB2, tamari, date paste, lime juice, garlic, ginger, and sriracha. Add the water 1 tablespoon at a time, whisking after each addition (up to 4 tablespoons) to make a smooth and creamy sauce.

MAKES 4 SERVINGS

Note: if you can't find defatted peanut flour or PB2, use two tablespoons of peanut or almond butter in this recipe instead of PB2 and use the larger amount of water. The recipe will contain more fat, but as long as you don't eat the sauce all day long, you'll be fine!

Raw Pad Thai

Pad Thai is just about everyone's favorite noodle dish at Thai restaurants. I've missed Thai food since going vegan because all the nearby Thai restaurants use fish sauce. I've made a raw version of pad Thai here with a super-tasty sauce that is fish-free. This dish makes a perfect light summer dinner. If you want to eat this in the cold of winter, feel free to briefly stir-fry the vegetables and lightly warm the sauce. The dish will no longer be raw, obviously, but will still be nutritious. Look for tamarind paste in the Asian section of your grocery store, in Asian markets, or online.

RAW NOODLES AND VEGETABLES

4 medium zucchini, shaved into very thin ribbons with a vegetable peeler, cut into matchsticks, or spiralized

4 medium carrots, shaved into thin ribbons with a vegetable peeler, cut into matchsticks, or spiralized

1 cup shredded red cabbage

2 cups small broccoli florets

1 red bell pepper, cut into 1/4-inch slices

1 cup fresh bean sprouts

1/4 cup roughly chopped fresh cilantro

1/4 cup roughly chopped fresh basil

1/4 cup roughly chopped fresh mint

1 small bunch scallions, cut into 1/4 inch slices

1 small jalapeño, minced

1/4 cup finely chopped raw cashews, for topping

PAD THAI SAUCE

1/4 cup raw tahini

1/2 cup fresh orange juice

2 tablespoons lime juice

1/4 cup Date Paste (page 16)

1/4 cup tamari or Bragg's Liquid Aminos

3 tablespoons finely minced ginger

1 medium clove garlic, minced

1/4 cup tamarind paste, optional

Arrange the zucchini, carrots, red cabbage, broccoli florets, red bell pepper, bean sprouts, cilantro, basil, mint, scallions, and jalapeño on 4 dinner plates or large shallow bowls. Sprinkle with the cashews.

In a blender, combine the tahini, orange juice, lime juice, date paste, tamari, ginger, garlic, and tamarind paste, if using. Blend the ingredients until fully combined and creamy, about 1 minute.

Evenly drizzle the sauce over the vegetables and serve immediately.

MAKES 4 SERVINGS

Cheesy Herb and Vegetable Crust Pizza

This recipe is fantastic for pizza night. You can use the toppings below or top with your own favorite vegetables. If you'd like to save time, you can cut corners by using a store-bought low-oil pizza sauce and having a batch of Fresh Vegan Moxarella (page 16) ready to go in your fridge. By the way, this pizza crust is yeast-free and gluten-free. You can double the crust recipe and freeze the additional crusts to have a head start on dinner on a busy night. Serve these pizzas with a side salad such as a crisp green salad dressed with Rich Balsamic Vinaigrette (page 92) or Creamy Vegan Ranch Dressing (page 91). (See photo on page 162.)

CHEESY HERB AND VEGETABLE CRUST
2 cups finely chopped cauliflower florets
1/2 cup Somer's All-Purpose Gluten-Free Flour (page 14)
1/2 cup chickpea flour (besan)
1 small carrot, shredded
1 medium clove garlic, finely minced
2 tablespoons minced dry-pack sun-dried tomatoes
1 teaspoon baking powder
1 teaspoon Italian seasoning
1 teaspoon no-salt seasoning blend, such as Mrs. Dash
1/2 teaspoon sea salt
2 tablespoons nutritional yeast
2 tablespoons ground golden flaxseed
1/2 cup water
1 cup loosely packed chopped fresh baby spinach

Preheat the oven to 400°F. Line two baking sheets with parchment paper or Silpat baking mats. In a food processor, combine the cauliflower and both flours. Pulse 10 to 15 times or until the cauliflower is the size of white rice grains. Add the carrot, garlic, sun dried tomatoes, baking powder, Italian seasonings, no-salt seasoning, salt, nutritional yeast, flaxseed, and water. Process until the dough sticks together, then gently fold in or pulse in the spinach to keep the dough from turning completely green all the way through.

Remove the dough from the food processor and divide it into four pieces. It will be quite wet, but do not be tempted to add more flour: the flax will thicken it up as it bakes! Using wet hands, shape each piece of dough into a 6 to 8-inch circular crust on a large baking sheet lined with a Silpat mat or parchment paper. Two pizzas should fit on each sheet.

Bake for 12 to 15 minutes, or until the crust feels firm and dry to the touch, rotating the baking sheets halfway through the baking time for even baking. Remove the crusts from the oven and set aside while you make the pizza sauce.

PIZZA SAUCE

1/4 cup vegetable broth
3 medium cloves garlic, minced
1 (14-ounce) can crushed tomatoes
1/2 teaspoon dried thyme
1/2 teaspoon dried oregano
1/2 teaspoon dried basil
1 teaspoon agave or pure maple syrup
1/2 teaspoons sea salt (or to taste)
1/4 teaspoon ground black pepper

Heat the broth in a small saucepan over medium heat. Add the garlic and sauté it for 1 to 2 minutes. Stir in the tomatoes, thyme, oregano, basil, agave, salt, and pepper. Reduce heat to low and allow the sauce to simmer and reduce in volume while you make the Fresh Vegan Moxarella.

TOPPING OPTIONS

Fresh Vegan Moxarella (page 16)
1/2 cup red or green bell pepper, cut into 1/8-inch slices
1/2 cup zucchini, cut into 1/8-inch slices
1/2 cup button mushrooms, cut into 1/8 inch slices
1/2 cup water-packed artichoke heart pieces
1/2 cup red onion, cut into 1/8-inch rings
1 to 2 Roma tomatoes, cut in to 1/8-inch slices
1/2 cup loosely packed fresh basil, roughly chopped
Other fresh vegetables of your choosing

Assembly: Preheat the oven to 500°. Spread each prepared pizza crust with 1/4 of the pizza sauce. Top each pizza with dollops of the Moxarella and your favorite vegetables. Bake the individual pizzas for 10 to 12 minutes until the cheese and crusts are nicely browned. Watch the pizzas carefully to make sure they don't burn. Note: there is a very fine line between nicely browned and burnt, so watch your pizzas carefully. Sprinkle them with the chopped fresh basil right before serving.

MAKES 4 SERVINGS

Chiles Rellenos Casserole Bake with Smoky Chipotle Enchilada Sauce

I first tried Chiles Rellenos at a quaint Mexican restaurant at the Tlaquepaque Shopping Center in Sedona, Arizona. I've been hooked ever since! Recreating this dish without the use of eggs, cheese, or anything fried seemed too large a task, but I think you'll be pleasantly surprised with this healthy version. It is topped with my favorite homemade enchilada sauce. I hope you love it as much as I do! Note: This recipe includes instructions for a Pepper Jack variation of the Moxarella recipe.

FILLING

1 recipe Fresh Vegan Moxarella (page 16) (optionally made with an additional tablespoon nutritional yeast + 1/4 to 1/2 teaspoon red pepper flakes)

2 (7-ounce) cans whole fire-roasted green chilies, drained and rinsed

2 1/2 cups cold water

1 cup chickpea flour

1 teaspoon kala namak (black salt)

2 tablespoons nutritional yeast

SMOKY CHIPOTLE ENCHILADA SAUCE

1 teaspoon ground cumin

1 teaspoon chili powder

1 teaspoon cocoa powder

1/8 to 1/4 teaspoon ground chipotle powder

2 tablespoons Somer's All-Purpose Gluten-Free Flour Blend (page 14)

2 cups vegetable broth

1/4 teaspoon liquid smoke

2 tablespoons tomato paste

1 tablespoon almond butter

1/2 teaspoon sea salt, or to taste

1/4 cup Cashew Sour Cream (page 154), for garnish

Roughly chopped cilantro, for garnish

Preheat the oven to 350°F. Lightly oil an 8×8-inch baking dish. If making the Pepper Jack Moxarella for this recipe, , add 1 tablespoon nutritional yeast and 1/4 to 1/2 teaspoon red pepper flakes when blending the moxarella ingredients in the blender.

Stuff the chilies with equally divided amounts of the Moxarella. Layer the stuffed chilies in the baking dish. If you have leftover Moxarella, you can use it to top the enchilada sauce, so set it aside.

In a medium saucepan, beat the water, chickpea flour, kala namak, and nutritional yeast with a wire whisk until completely smooth. Cook over medium-high heat, stirring constantly, for 2 to 3 minutes or until the mixture starts to thicken. Quickly pour the filling over the stuffed chiles, carefully re-arranging the chilies with tongs if necessary. Bake for 20 minutes.

While the chiles are baking, make the enchilada sauce. Using a dry medium saucepan, toast the cumin, chili powder, cocoa powder, and ground chipotle powder over medium-high heat for 30 to 60 seconds. Add the gluten-free flour blend and toast for a minute more until all is golden. Slowly whisk in the vegetable broth and liquid smoke, then the tomato paste and almond butter. Continue cooking and stirring until it comes to a boil and is slightly thickened. Season with salt to taste. Remove from heat and set aside.

Carefully remove the baking dish from the oven and top with the prepared enchilada sauce and any remaining Moxarella. Bake for an additional 10 minutes or until the sauce is bubbly and the Moxarella is golden. Let set and cool for about 10 minutes before cutting. Serve with dollops of sour cream and sprinkle with cilantro.

MAKES 4 SERVINGS

Note: To simplify this recipe, you can use 2 (7-ounce) cans of diced green chilies instead of stuffing whole chilies. Stir them into the chickpea batter before cooking and fold bits of the Moxarella into the casserole before baking. Proceed with the enchilada sauce as directed above.

Cheesy Cauliflower and Potato Bake

In Utah, particularly in the Mormon culture, there is a dish called funeral potatoes that is served at nearly every funeral. The original funeral potato recipe contains grated or cubed potatoes, sour cream, cheese, butter, gelatinous cream-of-something soup, cornflakes coated in butter, and more cheese. The dish has enough artery-clogging cholesterol to put anyone in the grave, especially when you consider that it's generally paired with ham and a variety of other heavy, fat-laden foods. Don't even get me started on the frightening green gelatin salads that accompany it for dessert. I'll be the first to admit that this dish does not taste quite like those funeral potatoes. I'd like to think of this as a lighter and fresher version that doesn't leave you feeling like you need to take a nap afterwards.

FILLING

2 large russet potatoes (1 pound), peeled and cut into 1/2-inch dice

1 small head cauliflower, cut into small florets (4 heaped cups)

SAUCE

1/4 cup raw cashews (soaked 4 to 6 hours)

1 cup unsweetened almond milk

3 tablespoons tapioca starch

1 tablespoon mellow white miso

1 teaspoon smoked paprika

1 small garlic clove, minced

1 teaspoon sea salt (or to taste)

1 teaspoon onion powder

1 tablespoon apple cider vinegar

2 tablespoons tomato paste

1 tablespoon dry sherry (optional)

1/2 teaspoon ground mustard powder

3 tablespoons nutritional yeast

Dash of cayenne

Preheat the oven to 375°F. In a large pot, bring 6 to 8 cups of salted water to a boil over high heat. Add the potatoes and cauliflower, reduce the heat to medium, and boil for 10 minutes. Don't worry if the vegetables are still slightly firm, as they will continue cooking in the oven.

While the vegetables are cooking, make the cheesy sauce: In a blender or food processor, combine the cashews, almond milk, tapioca starch, miso, smoked paprika, garlic, salt, onion powder, vinegar, tomato paste, sherry, mustard powder, nutritional yeast, and cayenne and blend until completely smooth and creamy, 1 to 2 minutes.

Drain the potatoes and cauliflower in a colander. Arrange the cooked vegetables in a lightly oiled 9×9-inch square casserole dish. Pour the cheesy sauce over the vegetables, gently folding the sauce into the vegetables if necessary.

Bake for 45 to 50 minutes, or until the top is crusty and golden, the sauce is thickened, and the vegetables are completely cooked through.

MAKES 4 SERVINGS

Grilled Eggplant and Zucchini Lasagna

I first made this recipe with Kathy Hester's Lentil and Quinoa Bolognese, which is featured in one of her cookbooks. It was so delicious, but in the interest of saving time, this recipe uses bottled sauce to get dinner on the table just a bit faster. Since this lasagna does not contain any pasta, it makes a super healthy dinner option. But don't worry about being hungry after eating this veggie-packed meal, as the portions sizes are huge.

- 2 small eggplants, sliced into 1/2 inch-rounds
- 4 medium zucchini, sliced lengthwise into 1/4-inch strips
- 1 large red onion, cut into 1/4-inch rings
- Salt and freshly ground pepper, to taste
- 1 (32-ounce) jar marinara sauce (look for a low- or no-oil variety)
- 1/2 cup cooked quinoa (See Notes)
- 1/2 cup cooked lentils (see Notes)
- 3 large Roma tomatoes, cut into 1/4-inch slices
- 1 recipe Fresh Vegan Moxarella, (page 16)

Preheat the oven to 400°F. In a large bowl, combine the eggplant, zucchini, and onion. Sprinkle the vegetables liberally with salt and pepper. Toss thoroughly. Grill the vegetables on a preheated outdoor grill or large cast iron skillet grill over medium-high heat for about 4 minutes on each side. You may need to use a bit of pan spray to keep them from sticking. The vegetables should still be fairly crisp, but have nice grill marks on them. Set the grilled vegetables aside until they are cool enough to handle.

Lightly oil a 9x13-inch casserole dish with cooking spray. In a large bowl, combine the cooked quinoa, lentils, and marinara sauce and stir to mix well. Add one cup of the sauce mixture to the casserole dish, spreading it evenly over the bottom.

Layer the half of the eggplant, zucchini, onion, and tomatoes over the sauce, then cover with half of the remaining sauce mixture. Dot half of the Moxarella over this layer. Layer with the remaining eggplant, zucchini, onion, and tomatoes, saving a few of the tomatoes to decorate the top. Spread the remaining sauce evenly over the top of the vegetables. Dollop the remaining half of the Moxarella on top and arrange the remaining tomato slices on top.

Bake for 30 to 35 minutes, or until bubbly and heated through. If desired, you can then broil it at 500° for 2 to 3 minutes or until the Moxarella gets a lovely brown crust. Let the lasagna cool for 10 to 15 minutes before slicing to firm up.

SERVES 4

Notes: If using an indoor grill pan/skillet, grilling the vegetables may be time consuming unless it is very large. If it isn't, I recommend broiling them instead. You won't get quite the same smoky taste that grilling gives, but this dish will still be delicious. To broil the vegetables, assemble the eggplant, zucchini, and onion on a large rimmed baking sheet lined with foil. Broil the vegetables on high for 5 minutes or until they start to brown, then flip them and broil for 5 minutes on the other side. Proceed with the recipe as directed.

If you don't have precooked quinoa and lentils, you can begin cooking them before you prepare the rest of this dish. In a small saucepan, combine 1/4 cup lentils with 1 cup of water. Bring them to a boil, then cover the saucepan and reduce the heat to a simmer. Let the lentils cook for 15 minutes. After 15 minutes, add 1/4 cup well-rinsed quinoa. Stir the pot, then cover and cook for 15 minutes more. At the end of the cooking time your lentils may still be a bit firm, but they will finish cooking in oven while the lasagna is baking.

Healthier Shepherd's Pie

I was first introduced to Shepherd's Pie while visiting Australia before I moved there to attend university. Classic Shepherd's Pie uses ground beef and an assortment of vegetables in a gravy-like sauce, all baked into a pastry crust and topped with mashed potatoes. It is comfort food at its finest! In creating a lighter, vegan version of the original, I skip the pastry and use hearty lentils, walnuts, and mushrooms to replace the traditional meat filling.

3/4 cup dry French green lentils, picked over and rinsed

1/4 cup raw walnuts, finely chopped

2 cups water

1 large head cauliflower, broken into small florets (about 6 cups)

1/4 cup vegetable broth

1 1/2 cups chopped white onion

2 medium carrots, cut into 1/4-inch dice

8 ounces button mushrooms, cut into 1/4-inch dice

2 medium cloves garlic, minced

2 cups fresh baby spinach, cut into 1/4-inch ribbons

1/2 cup frozen baby peas

2 tablespoons tomato paste

1 tablespoon nutritional yeast

2 tablespoons Somer's All-Purpose Gluten-Free Flour Blend (page 14)

2 tablespoons tamari or Bragg Liquid Aminos

1 teaspoon dried thyme

1 teaspoon mustard powder

1 tablespoon dry sherry

1 1/2 teaspoons sea salt, divided

1/2 teaspoon ground black pepper, divided

1/2 cup Cashew Sour Cream (page 154)

1/4 cup unsweetened almond milk

1 teaspoon nutritional yeast

Combine the lentils, walnuts, and water in a small saucepan. Cover and bring to a boil over medium-high heat. Once the water reaches a boil, reduce the heat to medium-low and simmer for 30 minutes, or until the lentils are mostly tender and cooked through. It's okay if they still have a bit of a toothy bite, as they will continue to cook in the oven.

While the lentils and walnuts are simmering, steam the cauliflower for 15 to 20 minutes, or until fork tender. Preheat the oven to 350°F.

Heat the broth in a medium-sized nonstick skillet over medium heat. Add the onion and carrots and sauté for 3 to 5 minutes. When the onion starts to become translucent, add the mushrooms and cook until they release their liquid, 3 to 5 minutes. Add the garlic and sauté for 1 to 2 minutes longer. Add the cooked lentils and walnuts, spinach, peas, tomato paste, nutritional yeast, flour blend, tamari-, thyme, mustard, sherry, 1 teaspoon of the salt, and the ¼ teaspoon of black pepper, stirring while cooking to incorporate all of the ingredients. Add 1 to 2 tablespoons of vegetable broth if the mixture seems too dry. Set aside.

Once the cauliflower has softened, transfer it to a food processor with the Cashew Sour Cream, almond milk, nutritional yeast, remaining 1/2 teaspoon salt, and remaining 1/4 teaspoon black pepper. Process the topping for several minutes until smooth and creamy.

Transfer the filling mixture to a lightly oiled 9-inch pie plate and smooth the top surface. Top with the cauliflower mash and distribute evenly until all the filling is covered. Bake for 30 to 35 minutes, or until heated through. If desired, broil the top for a few minutes until golden.

MAKES 4 SERVINGS

Homestyle Mexican Casserole

This south-of-the-border dish creates a fiesta in your mouth. The fast Nacho Cheesy Sauce is baked right into the casserole and is super tasty. You may find yourself cooking up a batch of the sauce to serve over steamed vegetables. Feel free to adjust the heat to your personal preference; I've kept the recipe mild here so kids and adults alike will enjoy it.

FILLING
1/4 cup vegetable broth
1 1/2 cups chopped onion
1 large red bell pepper, cut into 1/4-dice
1 large green bell pepper, cut into 1/4-inch dice
1 1/2 cups frozen organic corn
1 (15.5-ounce) can black beans, drained and rinsed
1 (14.5-ounce) can diced tomatoes, undrained (use Rotel brand for a spicier casserole)
1 cup cooked brown rice or quinoa
1/2 cup roughly chopped fresh cilantro

NACHO CHEESY SAUCE
1/4 cup raw cashew pieces, soaked for 4 hours
1 cup unsweetened almond milk
1 medium red bell pepper, roughly chopped
3 tablespoons tapioca starch
1 tablespoon mellow white miso
1 teaspoon smoked paprika
1 small garlic clove, minced
2 tablespoons lime juice
2 tablespoons nutritional yeast
1 tablespoon chili powder
1 tablespoon sriracha
1 heaped teaspoon ground cumin
1 teaspoon dried oregano
1 teaspoon sea salt, or to taste

GARNISH
1/4 cup Cashew Sour Cream (page 154)
Roughly chopped cilantro
Fire-Roasted Salsa (page 155)
Diced Roma tomatoes

Preheat the oven to 350°F. Heat the broth in a large skillet over medium heat. Add the onion and bell peppers and sauté until the onion is translucent, about 5 minutes. Add the corn, black beans, tomatoes, rice, and cilantro. Stir until heated through. Remove from heat and set aside.

In a blender, combine the cashews, almond milk, red bell pepper, tapioca starch, miso, smoked paprika, garlic, lime juice, nutritional yeast, chili powder, sriracha, cumin, oregano, and salt. Blend until completely smooth and creamy, 1 to 2 minutes. Set aside.

Lightly oil a 9x13-inch casserole dish. Add the filling ingredients. Pour the sauce over the filling ingredients, folding the sauce into the filling with a spoon. Bake for 45 to 50 minutes or until the top is golden and the sauce is thickened. Serve with dollops of Cashew Sour Cream, cilantro, salsa, and tomatoes.

MAKES 4 SERVINGS

Roasted Tofu and Vegetable Stir-Fry with Garlic-Ginger Sauce

My favorite Chinese restaurant dish is the house-special tofu with crisp vegetables and a flavorful sauce. I've tried to recreate that sort of dish here for an easy weeknight meal that's faster than picking up take-out and just as good without the deep-fried calorie bomb.

TOFU

14-ounces extra-firm tofu, drained, blotted dry, and cut into 1-inch cubes

2 tablespoons tamari or Bragg Liquid Aminos

GARLIC-GINGER SAUCE

1/2 cup water

1 tablespoon tamari or Bragg Liquid Aminos

1 tablespoon agave nectar or pure maple syrup

1 1/2 tablespoons non-GMO cornstarch or arrowroot

1 tablespoon mirin or seasoned rice vinegar

1 teaspoon toasted sesame oil

1 large clove garlic, minced

1/2 tablespoon finely minced ginger

1 teaspoon sea salt

1/4 teaspoon red pepper flakes or 1/4 teaspoon ground white pepper

VEGETABLES

2 tablespoons vegetable broth

1 large head broccoli cut into small florets (4 to 6 cups)

2 red bell peppers cut into 1/2-inch strips or one inch squares

2 large carrots, cut into 1/4-inch slices on the diagonal

2 cups fresh sugar snap peas or snow peas

2 ribs celery, cut diagonally into 1/4-inch slices

1 medium zucchini, sliced into 1/2 inch rounds

1 medium yellow squash, sliced into 1-inch cubes

1 large bunch green onions (scallions), cut into 1 1/2-inch pieces

Tofu: Preheat the oven to 475°F. Combine the tofu and tamari in a large bowl and toss gently to coat so that the sauce is evenly distributed. Arrange the tofu pieces on a Silpat mat or parchment-lined large rimmed baking sheet. Bake the tofu for 15 to 20 minutes while you make the sauce and cook the vegetables.

Sauce: In a small bowl, combine the water, tamari, agave, cornstarch, mirin, sesame oil, garlic, ginger, salt, and red pepper flakes. Whisk all of the ingredients together until well combined. Set aside.

Vegetables: Heat the broth in a large nonstick skillet over medium-high heat. Add the broccoli, bell pepper, carrots, sugar snap peas, celery, zucchini, and yellow squash. Sauté the vegetables for 2 to 3 minutes, stirring occasionally, until they are crisp-tender (on the crisper side). Add the reserved sauce and cook over high heat for 1 to 2 minutes. Divide the vegetables among four large plates and serve topped with the tofu.

MAKES 4 SERVINGS

Notes: Chinese food is super salty and often seasoned with the flavor enhancer MSG. If you find this recipe isn't salty enough to satisfy your take-out craving, increase the salt in the recipe by another 1/4 or 1/2 teaspoon. It will be a high sodium dish, so be mindful if you have high blood pressure. This recipe may be served over your favorite grain, such as brown rice or quinoa (1/2 cup cooked grain per person), or even over "cauliflower or parsnip rice" as instructed in the Cauliflower or Parsnip Tabbouleh recipe (page 120). In our family, we like to eat the vegetables and tofu straight up.

Stir-Fry Variations

As with most stir-fry dishes, this recipe is completely open to interpretation and is a good way to use up whatever vegetables you have in your crisper.

- If you like a sweeter stir-fry sauce, add a couple of tablespoons of Date Paste (page 15) to the sauce mixture before whisking.
- For a spicier sauce, increase the red pepper flakes or ground white pepper to 1/2 teaspoon or one full teaspoon.
- To make this recipe into a rich garlic sauce, increase the garlic to 3 to 5 cloves and add an additional tablespoon or two of Braggs or tamari.
- For a Kung Pao stir-fry, add the following to your sauce before whisking: 2 tablespoons date paste, 1/2 to 1 teaspoon red pepper flakes, 3 to 5 cloves of garlic, and 1 to 2 additional tablespoons of tamari. To finish the presentation, add a tablespoon of roughly chopped roasted peanuts or cashews over each dish.

"Cowboy Special" One-Pot Pasta

Growing up my mom made this great one-pot pasta dish called Cowboy Special. It was easy, fast, and awesome—we all loved it to bits. This is my vegan rendition of that dish.

7 ounces brown rice elbow macaroni

2 1/2 cups vegetable broth

1 (14.5-ounce) can petite diced tomatoes, undrained

1 tablespoon almond butter

1 cup red onion, cut into 1/4-inch dice

1 medium zucchini, cut into 1/2-inch dice (about 2 cups)

2 to 3 cloves garlic, thinly sliced

1 cup cooked or canned Great Northern beans, drained and rinsed

1 teaspoon dried oregano

1/8 teaspoon red pepper flakes

1 teaspoon sea salt, or to taste

1/2 teaspoon ground black pepper

1/4 cup roughly chopped basil

In a medium-sized lidded pot, combine the pasta, broth, tomatoes, almond butter, onion, zucchini, garlic, beans, oregano, red pepper flakes, salt, and black pepper. Bring the ingredients to a boil over high heat, then cover with the lid and reduce the heat to a simmer over medium-low heat. Cook for 15 to 18 minutes, or until most of the liquid is absorbed and the pasta is soft. Stir in the fresh basil just before serving.

MAKES 4 SERVINGS

Note: My family also loves this dish with lentils instead of white beans, so if you have cooked lentils on hand, try them instead. If you prefer crisper zucchini (like I do), add it to the pot during the last few minutes of cooking rather than at the beginning.

Happiness in a Cookie Bite (page 188)

TWELVE

Desserts

LET'S FACE IT, LIFE IS SIMPLY SWEETER WITH DESSERT. The problem with desserts though is that most of us feel entitled to treat ourselves to something sweet far more often than we should. Instead of desserts being a special occasion thing, it's easy to fall into the pattern of dipping into that pint of ice cream every night or stealing just one more cookie out of the cookie jar.

Unfortunately, in addition to treats being consumed far too often by most of us, desserts are generally full of refined sugars, refined flours, and have a high fat content or are just downright unhealthy.

So, I've created a bunch of desserts that are actually good for you. Now hang on a second, that doesn't mean I'm giving you a license to eat dessert every day. Michael Pollan, my favorite veg-curious omnivore recommends only eating desserts on special occasions, or on days that start with an "S." I'm asking you to follow those same guidelines. So save the treats for the weekend or for that special occasion and watch your waistline shrink.

Accidental Overnight Dark Chocolate Pudding

This recipe was one of those happy accidents where I was interrupted after making a smoothie for my family and I stuck the smoothie in the fridge, thinking it would still be good the next day. But something magical occurred overnight. The dessert solidified and turned into chocolate pudding. Best happy accident!

- 2 1/2 cups unsweetened soy milk
- 3 medium bananas
- 1/4 cup unsweetened cocoa powder
- 1/4 cup Justin's Chocolate Hazelnut Butter or natural peanut butter
- 1 tablespoon pure maple syrup
- 1/4 teaspoon powdered stevia, or to taste

In a blender, combine the soy milk, bananas, cocoa powder, chocolate hazelnut butter, maple syrup, and stevia. Blend until completely smooth and creamy, about one minute. Divide the mixture evenly among 4 dessert bowls. Refrigerate for several hours or overnight.

MAKES 4 SERVINGS

Blueberry Peach Tart with Apricot Crumble

This crumble is one of my favorite things. Ever. It tastes indulgent but is full of goodness. It presents beautifully, too. To serve this to company, double the recipe and use an 8-inch springform pan.

1/2 cup Somer's All-Purpose Gluten-Free Flour Blend (page 14)
3 tablespoons raw cashew pieces
5 soft, pitted medjool dates
5 dried apricot halves
1/2 teaspoon vanilla extract
1/8 teaspoon powdered stevia
2 tablespoons water
Pinch sea salt
1/2 teaspoon ground cinnamon
2 to 3 medium-sized peaches, pitted and thinly sliced (with skins on)
1/2 cup fresh or frozen blueberries

Preheat the oven to 350°F. In a food processor, combine the flour, cashews, dates, apricots, vanilla, stevia, water, salt, and cinnamon. Process the mixture until it is fine and crumbly. Press half of the crumb mixture into the bottom of a 6-inch springform pan. The mixture will be a bit dry, but the juices from the fruit will moisten it while it's baking. Top with a layer of sliced peaches and place the blueberries evenly over the top. Sprinkle the remaining crumble dough over the top. Bake for 25 to 30 minutes, or until fragrant and the crumble is golden. Let the dessert cool for 10 minutes, then remove it from the pan and it let cool slightly before serving.

MAKES 4 SERVINGS

Note: Plums make a nice substitute for the peaches when they are in season.

Happiness in a Cookie Bite

This "healthy cookie" recipe is adapted from one my friend Erika makes. When she brought them over one day for a ladies' lunch, none of us could stop eating them or wipe the smiles off our faces! This recipe adaptation is used with permission. (Also see photo on page 184.)

1/2 cup rolled oats

1/4 cup unsweetened almond butter or nut butter of choice

2 tablespoons pure maple syrup

1/4 cup unsweetened shredded coconut flakes

2 tablespoons ground golden flaxseed

2 tablespoons mini vegan chocolate chips (I like Lily's stevia-sweetened or Enjoy Life)

1/2 teaspoon vanilla extract

1/4 teaspoon ground cinnamon

Pinch sea salt (to taste)

In a large bowl, combine the rolled oats, almond butter, maple syrup, coconut, flaxseed, chocolate chips, vanilla, cinnamon, and salt. Mix the ingredients using your hands to combine everything thoroughly. Add water, 1 teaspoon at a time, if the batter seems too dry. Roll the dough with wet hands into 1-inch balls and arrange them on a plate. Cover and refrigerate up to 1 week.

MAKES 4 SERVINGS

Note: If you aren't a chocolate lover, try raisins, dried cherries, and cranberries or chopped dried apricots instead of chocolate and up the cinnamon by another 1/4 teaspoon.

Chocolate Chip Mini-Blondie Muffins

Once upon a time, I counted calories. I used to buy those 100-calorie snack packs of mini cupcakes or muffins as a reward for myself. I knew they were absolute junk and filled with chemicals, but dieting was hard and I wanted to eat something that would fit my calorie requirements and fulfil my sweet tooth. So I kept buying them. These mini blondie muffins are the answer to that dilemma.

3/4 cup Somer's All-Purpose Gluten-Free Flour Blend (page 14)
1 tablespoon ground golden flaxseed
1/2 teaspoon baking powder
1/4 teaspoon stevia powder
Pinch sea salt
2 tablespoons agave nectar or pure maple syrup
1 tablespoon Date Paste (page 16)
2 tablespoons unsweetened applesauce
2 tablespoons almond milk
1/4 teaspoon apple cider vinegar
1 teaspoon vanilla extract
2 tablespoons vegan mini chocolate chips (I like Lily's stevia-sweetened or Enjoy Life)

Preheat the oven to 350°F. Combine the gluten-free flour, ground flax, baking powder, stevia and salt in a medium bowl with a wire whisk. Add the agave, applesauce, almond milk, vinegar, vanilla, and chocolate chips. Stir the batter until just combined. Using a tablespoon, scoop the batter into a lightly oiled nonstick mini-muffin tin. You should end up with 12 muffins. Bake for 10 to 12 minutes.

MAKES 4 SERVINGS

Note: This recipe is also delicious with 1 teaspoon of lemon zest and 1/2 cup of fresh blueberries added instead of the chocolate chips.

Chocolate-Orange Silk Mousse

This recipe is adapted from one shared with me from my running buddy Christina. She's not vegan, but this recipe is based on one of her favorite desserts. I've taken out the refined sugars and added some tastiness in the form of the orange flavoring for a chocolate mousse that'll have you wondering how it could possibly be vegan or healthy.

1 (12-ounce) package Mori-Nu (or other brand) silken tofu
1/4 cup mini vegan chocolate chips (I like Lily's stevia-sweetened or Enjoy Life)
1/3 cup unsweetened cocoa powder
1/4 cup boiling water
1 teaspoon vanilla extract
1/2 teaspoon freshly grated orange zest
1/4 cup raw cashew pieces (soaked for 4 to 6 hours)
1/2 cup packed soft medjool dates, pitted (soaked for 3 hours)
1/4 teaspoon stevia powder, or to taste

In a high-speed blender or food processor, combine the tofu, chocolate chips, cocoa powder, boiling water, vanilla, orange zest, cashews, dates, and stevia powder. Process until the mixture is completely smooth and creamy, 1 to 2 minutes. Add water a tablespoon at a time if it is difficult to blend. Divide the mousse into 4 ramekins or small glass bowls. Refrigerate to chill for 60 minutes or overnight.

MAKES 4 SERVINGS

Easy Applesauce Snack Cake

The day I came up with the recipe for this cake was like a Eureka moment. It is so simple, yet so good. Also, the serving size is a pretty big piece of cake, which is awesome. I think every single one of my testers made this cake in an excited recipe tester frenzy. All of them enjoyed it and I hope you will too! This is lovely decorated with a thinly sliced apple on top before baking.

> 1 1/2 cups Somer's All-Purpose Gluten-Free Flour Blend (page 14)
> 1 tablespoon baking powder
> 1/4 teaspoon sea salt
> 1/4 teaspoon powdered stevia
> 1 teaspoon ground cinnamon
> 1/2 cup water
> 1/2 cup unsweetened applesauce
> 1/2 cup Date Paste (page 16)
> 1 teaspoon vanilla extract

Preheat the oven to 350°F. Lightly oil an 8x4-inch loaf pan and set aside. In a large bowl, combine the flour, baking powder, salt, stevia, and cinnamon. Mix with a wire whisk and set aside.

In a medium bowl, combine the water, applesauce, date paste, and vanilla. Stir the wet ingredients until smooth. Add the liquid ingredients to the dry ingredients and fold together until the batter is just combined.

Pour the batter into the prepared pan. Bake for 35 to 40 minutes or until the cake is golden brown and a toothpick comes out clean. Remove the cake from the pan and let cool for a bit before slicing.

MAKES 4 SERVINGS

Notes: This recipe originally started out as muffins. If you'd like to make muffins, simply fill a lightly oiled or paper-lined muffin tin 2/3 full of batter. You will get 10 to 12 muffins from this recipe. Don't overfill, or they will expand over the edge of the muffin shape. Bake at 350°F for 20 to 25 minutes, or until golden brown and a toothpick comes out clean.

No Bake, No Stovetop Cookie Bites

When I was growing up, my mom made these great no-bake cookies all the time as an afterschool snack. They were super delicious and full of oats, chocolate, and peanut butter. Such a good combination! However, the recipe also had a stick of margarine and loads of sugar, making this a treat I haven't made as often for my own kids. One day I was trying to make a raw-ish brownie out of dates, nuts, and chocolate. Instead, my creation tasted just like those no-bake cookies I loved so much as a child. I couldn't have been happier about my kitchen mishap. My testers also adored these cookie bites. I think you will, too.

1/2 cup raw cashews, almonds or walnuts (or a combination)

1/2 cup gluten-free rolled oats

3/4 cup pitted soft medjool dates (roughly chopped after measuring, packed into a measuring cup)

Pinch sea salt

3/4 teaspoon vanilla extract

1 tablespoon unsweetened cocoa powder

2 tablespoons vegan dark chocolate chips

1 tablespoon natural peanut butter

1 tablespoon agave nectar or pure maple syrup

In a food processor, combine the nuts, oats, dates, salt, vanilla, cocoa powder, chocolate chips, peanut butter, and maple syrup. Process until finely crumbled. Continue processing until the mixture starts to hold together into a mass. If your mixture seems dry, add water 1 teaspoon at a time until it adheres.

With wet hands, press the dough into an 8x4-inch loaf pan lined with parchment paper. Refrigerate the dough until firm. Remove the parchment and the chilled dough from the loaf pan and cut into 1-inch x 1-inch cookie pieces. These cookies keep nicely well-wrapped in the refrigerator for up to 10 days or in the freezer for up to 3 months.

MAKES 4 SERVINGS

Luscious Creamy Lemon Tarts

Desserts made with lemon make me swoon. This one is no exception. The refreshing tartness of the lemon combined with the lush and creamy filling over a healthy pastry crust makes life so much sweeter!

CRUSTS
1/2 cup Somer's All-Purpose Gluten-Free Flour Blend (page 14)
1/4 cup raw cashew pieces
1/4 cup dried pineapple
Pinch sea salt
2 tablespoons water, or more if needed

FILLING
Juice and zest of 1 medium lemon
1 (12.3-ounce) package Mori-Nu firm silken tofu
1/4 cup coconut butter, at room temperature (not coconut oil)
1/4 cup agave nectar or brown rice syrup
1/4 teaspoon powdered stevia, or to taste

Preheat the oven to 350°F. In a high-speed blender or a mini-food processor, combine the flour, cashews, dried pineapple, and salt. Pulse or process the mixture until very fine and crumbly. Add water as necessary to make a stiff dough.

Divide the dough among four (1/2 cup) ramekins or mini tart pans, pressing the mixture down with your fingers make a base.

Place the ramekins on a baking sheet and bake the crusts for 12 to 15 minutes, or until lightly golden.

While the crust is baking, make the filling. In a food processor or high speed blender, combine the lemon zest, lemon juice, tofu, coconut butter, agave, and powdered stevia. Blend until the mixture is smooth and creamy. Adjust the sweetness to taste if necessary. Divide the filling among the 4 ramekins or mini tart dishes. Chill for an hour or two, until set.

MAKES 4 SERVINGS

Nice Creams

Some genius discovered that frozen processed bananas actually make a crazy-convincing and delicious stand-in for soft-serve ice cream. I would credit that person if I could actually figure out who it was. The vegan community has lovingly bestowed the name "Nice Cream" on the blended concoction. Combinations with frozen bananas are endless, and I'm sure in no time you will be recreating your most loved flavors, but here are just a handful of my favorites that will more than satisfy that weekend ice cream craving.

Chocolate Peanut Butter Cup Soft-Serve

Almost everyone loves peanut butter and chocolate. Here that favorite combination gets made into a delicious nice cream!

- 4 medium-sized bananas, cut into 1-inch pieces and frozen
- 2 tablespoons unsweetened cocoa powder
- 2 tablespoons natural peanut butter
- 2 tablespoons mini vegan chocolate chips
- 1 tablespoon to 1/4 cup unsweetened almond milk, as needed

In a food processor, process the frozen banana pieces, cocoa powder, and peanut butter until smooth and creamy. Add the almond milk one tablespoon at a time as necessary for processing. (The more frozen solid your bananas are, the more almond milk you might need.) Pulse in the chocolate chips. Serve immediately.

MAKES 4 SERVINGS

Chunky Monkey Soft-Serve

Chunky Monkey is another Ben and Jerry's past favorite flavor of mine reinvented so that you can continue to enjoy the delicious flavor combination.

    4 medium-sized bananas, cut into 1-inch pieces and frozen
    1 tablespoon to 1/4 cup unsweetened almond milk, as needed
    1/4 cup chopped raw walnut pieces
    2 tablespoons mini vegan chocolate chips

In a food processor, process the frozen banana pieces until smooth and creamy, adding almond milk one tablespoon at a time as necessary for processing. Add the walnuts and chocolate chips and pulse until evenly distributed. Serve immediately.

MAKES 4 SERVINGS

Raw Almond and Pistachio Ice Cream

This tasty almond and pistachio nice cream gets its lovely green color from spinach; however, no one will know it's in there if you don't tell them!

    4 medium-sized bananas, cut into 1-inch pieces and frozen
    1 medium, barely ripe Hass avocado, peeled, pitted, cut into 1/2-inch dice, and frozen
    1/2 cup packed fresh baby spinach
    2 tablespoons agave nectar or pure maple syrup
    1/4 teaspoon pure almond extract
    1 tablespoon to 1/4 cup unsweetened almond milk, as needed
    2 tablespoons roughly chopped raw pistachios
    Pinch of powdered stevia, or to taste

In a food processor, process the frozen banana pieces, avocado, spinach, agave, and almond extract until smooth and creamy, adding almond milk one tablespoon at a time as necessary for processing. Add the pistachios and pulse until combined. Taste for sweetness and add stevia if desired. Serve immediately.

MAKES 4 SERVINGS

Cherry Garcia Soft-Serve

It's no secret that in my pre-vegan days Ben and Jerry's ice cream was my very favorite brand. Cherry Garcia held a special place in my heart, and I can enjoy it still without guilt with this delicious diet-friendly soft serve.

- **4 medium-sized bananas, cut into 1-inch pieces and frozen**
- **1 cup frozen cherries**
- **1/2 teaspoon vanilla extract**
- **1 tablespoon to 1/4 cup unsweetened almond milk, as needed**
- **2 tablespoons mini vegan chocolate chips**

In a food processor, process the frozen banana pieces, cherries, and vanilla until creamy, adding almond milk, one tablespoon at a time as necessary, for processing. Pulse in the chocolate chips. Serve immediately.

MAKES 4 SERVINGS

Thirteen

1-3-5 Day Bonus Juice Feast

I LOVE FRESH JUICE! It gives me an instant nutrition and energy boost and can sometimes give the body a much-needed break after unhealthy eating or consuming too many heavy foods. This chapter provides juice feast basics (which is a more awesome name for a juice fast) for juicing novices, as well as some fresh and tasty recipes for the seasoned juicer. These recipes are completely optional for users of *The Abundance Diet*, however they can be ideal for melting away additional pounds as a kick start or for finishing up the 28-day challenge.

A juice feast is a gentle cleanse regimen, lasting the duration that you choose,that consists of only juices. There are lots of reasons people choose to do a juice feast, such as to lose weight, to use the quickly absorbed nutrients, or to fight serious health issues. Sometimes people simply do the juice feast because they want to "reset" their bodies to regain lightness and mental clarity. I know there's a lot of debate about smoothies vs. juicing vs. neither, but I've found both green smoothies and juicing have their place in my lifestyle.

When juicing at home, I choose organic produce as much as possible so I can reduce pesticide concentration in my diet. If you can afford organic produce, I recommend that you do the same. If using conventional produce, you may want to peel your fruits or vegetables before juicing, especially any items on the "dirty dozen" list (page 206) of produce known to contain the most pesticides. (See the Environmental Working Group's "2015 Shopper's Guide to Pesticides in Produce" at www.ewg.org.)

All you really need to get started juicing are a juicer and some fresh produce. It's basically foolproof. If you already own a juicer, then you're ready to go. If you are considering purchasing a juicer, there are several kinds as well as many brands. The most common types are the masticating juicer and the centrifugal juicer.

Masticating juicers use a single auger function to extract the juice from the pulp. The juice is pressed through a screen and the pulp is expelled in a separate area of the juicer. Seasoned juicers will tell you that a masticating juicer is a better choice for preserving nutrients than a centrifugal juicer, since the juice is processed at a lower temperature and is less likely to oxidize as quickly. Masticating juicers typically operate more slowly than centrifugal juicers since time and care are needed to avoid overheating. These juicers can be purchased online, at a health food store, or at a specialty store.

Centrifugal juicers use a flat blade to cut the produce and a rapid spinning motion to propel the juice from the pulp. Because the centrifugal juicer operates at a higher speed, nutrients may be lost more quickly. Centrifugal juicers can usually be found at almost any big box store at a reasonable price for a low-end model. These juicers also have the benefit of speedy operation and sometimes are easier to clean than the masticating models.

The "Dirty" Dozen	
Buy these vegetables organic whenever possible, as the non-organic varieties are often heavily sprayed with chemicals.	
apples	spinach
peaches	sweet bell peppers
nectarines	cucumbers
strawberries	cherry tomatoes
grapes	snap peas (imported)
celery	potatoes

Important note: neither masticating nor centrifugal juicers are great for juicing wheatgrass. Typically, masticating juicers require a special part that has to be ordered to be effective for wheatgrass juicing. If you intend to juice wheatgrass, you may even want to consider purchasing a special juicer specifically designed for wheatgrass.

So which juicer is right for you? Well, that depends on your budget, how often you plan to juice, and many other variables. I own both a masticating juicer and a centrifugal juicer. The masticating juicer I own is a Champion brand. It's a higher-end juicer and it has shown its true colors: I've owned it for over 15 years and it still operates beautifully. The juice is very fresh, and I like that I can store it for up to 24 hours in a lidded jar without too much oxidation occurring. However, it takes time and care to make a reasonable amount of juice with this machine because the produce needs to be chopped into small enough pieces to fit into the chute. Also, I swear this machine weighs more than twenty pounds, so assembly can sometimes feel like arm-wrestling a bear. Clean-up can also be time consuming, since all removable washable parts require hand washing with mild detergent.

My centrifugal juicer is a Wide Mouth juicer made by Hamilton Beach. I bought it very inexpensively at my local big box store. I love that I can fit apples and other whole produce into the chute without having to chop it into pieces. The machine is speedy and efficient. I get nearly the same volume of juice as I do from my masticating juicer, and the leftover pulp is only slightly wetter. Clean up of this machine is easy and all washable parts are dishwasher safe, which is a bonus. However, I somehow doubt that this machine will still be in sturdy and efficient operation 15 years from now.

The juicer that works best for you will depend on your budget, health needs/goals, ease of use, and so on. I love both of my models for different reasons, so I'm sure whichever juicer you choose, it will be sufficient for your current needs.

Juice Feast Basics

Here are some things I want to share with you that I've gleaned from research as well as from doing my own juice feasts over the years.

Juicing in the morning. I'm more likely to stay on track if I get my juice supply ready for the day first thing in the morning. As I stated above, I have a masticating juicer and a centrifugal juicer. A masticating juicer can help your juice stay fresher longer with more nutrients, but even though it's best (in any case) to drink juice fresh right when you press it, there are ways you can minimize nutrient loss for juice pressed through either machine. Also, I recommend using as much organic produce as possible so you don't overload on concentrated pesticide residue.

Use lidded jars. Immediately store your freshly pressed juice in lidded glass jars such as mason jars, filled as closely to the top as possible to prevent oxidation, in the coldest part of your refrigerator.

Enjoy variety. Drink a variety of the juices in this chapter during the day in order to keep your palate happy and to have a new flavor to look forward to. In no time, you'll be creating your own juice recipes.

Wash your produce. Always make sure to wash produce well before juicing. Dirt and bugs are commonplace in many types of produce, so get it nice and clean before putting it through your machine.

The peeling option. Peeling your fruits and vegetables is entirely optional. A juicer can handle the skins of almost any fruit or vegetable. If you are using organic produce that is well washed, you can certainly leave the skins on. If using conventional produce, especially any produce on the "dirty dozen" list (page 227), you may want to peel your produce before juicing to reduce pesticide residue as much as possible.

Preserve with citrus. Add lemons or limes to your juices to help preserve them. Sometimes I leave the peel on, which makes the juice more intensely flavored, but other times I don't want that intense flavor, so I leave the peel off.

Drink as much juice as you'd like. I've found a schedule that works for me. I typically consume five to six juices (16 to 18 ounces per juice) a day and consume them 2 hours apart from 9:00 a.m. to 7:00 p.m. I don't get overly hungry or have energy loss. I like to strain my juices through a wire mesh strainer for very smooth juice without any traces of pulp, but that's my personal preference. You can leave yours unstrained if you prefer.

Nut milks. I also include nut milk in my daily juice regimen. I've found that it really takes the edge off my hunger and makes doing a juice feast just that much more doable. Obviously, nut milk isn't technically any type of juice, but it works well for me in conjunction with this type of "reset." I usually drink the nut milk in the evening or when I'm having my strongest cravings.

Favor veggies over fruits. Emphasize veggies as much as you can in the juice feast. Too many fruits while juicing isn't as beneficial as drinking lots of leafy greens and veggies. This is because an overconsumption of fruit juice can mess with your body's pH balance and send you into sugar overdrive.

Use purified water. Make sure to have as much purified water and unsweetened herbal tea as you like throughout the day.

Get plenty of rest. While doing your juice feast, you might find that you need a bit more sleep than normal.

You can do a 1-day, 3-day, or 5-day. If you have a lot of weight to lose and want to do an extended juice fast, you will need to do it under the supervision of a medical doctor. Joe Cross, the high-energy Australian from the documentary *Fat, Sick and Nearly Dead* demonstrated that more than 60 days of juicing put his autoimmune disease into remission and helped him lose all the excess weight he was carrying. However, he did the juice fast under the strict medical supervision of plant based guru, Dr. Joel Fuhrman. Since his juice fast, he's kept the weight off with continued juicing and a high percentage plant-based diet.

It's okay if you fall off the juice wagon. You can always climb back on until you reach your desired goal. Also, if for any reason you start to feel ill (more than just mild cleanse-associated headaches), stop the juice fast and consult a medical professional.

Juice Mindfully. While juicing can make you feel great, possible side effects of juice fasting can include feeling tired, mild headaches, sluggish system, light-headedness, and more during the duration of your cleanse. These side effects can occur because you're shedding lots of excess pounds and releasing toxins from your body. Make sure to get plenty of rest to help your body repair during the duration of the juice feast. Choose a time to start when you can be at home such as over the weekend or during an extended break instead of trying to do a juice fast through the work week. Use caution while driving and always be near a bathroom until you know how juicing affects you. Anyone, especially persons with weakened immune systems or other medical condition, should consult their physician before beginning a juice fast of any kind.

And finally, my method for doing a juice feast includes preparing several recipes in advance so that I'm not juicing all day long. I like to make my juices in the evening or the morning, and I typically prepare enough juice to last for a day or two so I don't get burned out. I always use the Ultra Green Juice (page 215) as the basis of my juice feast and add a couple of other juices to it during the day, finishing off with the Raw Cashew Horchata (page 216). If you prefer, you can prepare juices fresh throughout the day, although if you do so and don't have anyone joining you on your juice feast, you may want to consider dividing each recipe into individual servings so you have the freshest possible juice. Now, let's get juicing!

Minted Cucumber Melon Juice

I adore the combination of cucumber and melon. This recipe gets even fresher with mint, which makes it cooling and delicious. Organic melons can be juiced with peel and seeds intact, or you can remove the rind and seeds for improved flavor.

    1 firm medium-sized cantaloupe (ripe but not overly soft)
    4 large cucumbers
    1 cup fresh mint leaves
    1 small lime, peeled

Press all of your fruits and vegetables through your juicer. Strain the juice if desired. Stored in lidded glass jars, it will keep for up to two days.

MAKES 40 TO 50 OUNCES

Note: You can use any kind of melon you'd like in this juice. Fresh honeydew or watermelon would be lovely.

Depending on the quality of your juicer and the size of your produce, you may get more or less juice.

Better Than V8

I love V8, but the popular vegetable drink has nearly a whole day's worth of sodium. This recipe is better and fresher than the original, with no added salt.

  1/4 small red onion
  4 cups fresh baby spinach
  2 large cucumbers
  4 to 6 large celery ribs
  1 pound carrots
  8 to 10 ripe Roma tomatoes
  1 small beet, well-scrubbed (optional)
  Dash of cayenne (optional)

Press all of your vegetables through your juicer. Strain the juice if desired and add the optional cayenne (if using). Store in lidded glass jars for up to two days.

MAKES ABOUT 48 OUNCES (3 PINTS)

Note: Depending on the quality of your juicer and the size of your produce, you may get more or less juice.

Chia Limeade

This refreshing beverage gets its origins from the Tarahumara Indians in Copper Canyon, Mexico. The chia seeds add a bit of protein and fiber and help keep things moving in your digestive system. If you like, you can replace some of the water in this recipe and eliminate the stevia entirely by adding the fresh juice of one or two apples or firm pears.

2 cups purified water
juice of one small lime
1 tablespoon chia seeds
8-10 drops liquid stevia

Place the purified water, lime juice, chia seeds, and stevia in a tall glass or a mason jar. Stir briskly to combine. Let the chia limeade rest in the fridge for 20 to 30 minutes or until the chia seeds are nice and plump. You can also keep this in a lidded glass jar and shake it up to keep the seeds from settling to the bottom.

MAKES ABOUT 18 OUNCES

Orange Carrot Beet-It Juice

The vibrant color of this juice is so much fun, but the taste is even more interesting. Earthy and sweet with notes of citrus from the orange, nutrition from the beet greens, and a bit of spice from the ginger rounds it out nicely.

4 medium-sized navel oranges, peeled
4 medium beets, well-scrubbed
8 large carrots
4 to 8 beet green leaves
2 inch piece of fresh ginger

Press all of your fruits and vegetables through your juicer. Strain the juice if desired. Store in lidded glass jars for up to two days.

MAKES 30 TO 40 OUNCES

Note: Depending on the quality of your juicer and the size of your produce, you may get more or less juice.

Australian Carrot Apple Celery Refresher

This combination is super popular amongst Australians. Once you drink it, you'll understand why!

- **1 large bunch celery, washed and separated into ribs**
- **6 medium apples**
- **1 pound carrots**

Press all of your vegetables and fruits through your juicer. Strain the juice if desired. Store in lidded glass jars for up to two days.

MAKES ABOUT 48 OUNCES (3 PINTS)

Note: Depending on the quality of your juicer and the size of your produce, you may get more or less juice.

Savory Spicy-8 Juice

This juice isn't actually anything like a V8 juice, so if you are looking for that kind of juice, use my Better Than V8 juice on page 210. This juice has a bright orange color. It packs a powerful nutritional punch with a unique, savory blend of vegetables and a spicy metabolism-boosting hit from the jalapeño and garlic. This juice is loaded with beta-carotene, vitamin A, vitamin C, calcium, and iron. I find that drinking it provides a really great break from sweeter, fruit-based juices.

    6 large carrots
    5 medium-sized ripe tomatoes
    6 large ribs celery
    1 to 2 medium-sized parsnips
    1 small lemon, peeled
    1 medium-sized red bell pepper
    1/2 to 1 small jalapeño, seeded (omit for a less spicy juice)
    2 to 3 sprigs fresh parsley
    Optional: 1 clove garlic; 1 cup fresh greens; 1/2 small beet, well-scrubbed

Press all of your vegetables through your juicer. Strain the juice if desired. Store your juice in lidded glass containers, such as a mason jar.

MAKES 40 TO 50 OUNCES

Note: Depending on the quality of your juicer and the size of your produce, you may get more or less juice.

Ultra Green Juice

This juice is a great basis for the Juice Feast! It is filled with nutritious greens and has a perfect alkaline balance. You'll love having this very green and surprisingly tasty juice to energize you throughout the day. This recipe was created by my brother Curtis, an ultra-runner who has completed multiple 100-mile races in under 30 hours. I can't guarantee that you'll be able to do the same if you drink this, but it will certainly fuel your cells and put a zip in your step.

   4 cups packed baby spinach
   2 large cucumbers
   1 large bunch of celery, washed well and separated into ribs
   1 cup broccoli
   1 medium-sized bunch parsley
   3 to 6 medium-sized apples (use the greater amount if you prefer a sweeter juice)
   1 small lime, peeled
   1/2 small peeled lemon, peeled
   1 (1-inch) piece fresh ginger

Press all of your fruits and vegetables through your juicer. Strain the juice if desired. Juice is best stored in lidded glass jars.

MAKES ABOUT 64 OUNCES (4 PINTS)

Note: If you add 5 to 6 medium sized carrots to this juice, the juice turns an awesome army green color and gets a bit more sweetness along with additional vitamins. I typically consume this juice in tandem with one or two other juices in this chapter, plus the Cashew Horchata, to round out a day on the juice feast.

Depending on the quality of your juicer and the size of your produce, you may get more or less juice.

Raw Cashew Horchata

Horchata is a delicious beverage from Mexico that is typically made from rice milk, lots of sugar, and cinnamon. There are a few Mexican restaurants that serve a vegan version, but most often dairy is added. Here, I've created a raw version to enjoy on the juice feast. While this is not technically a juice recipe, it is possibly my favorite recipe in this chapter. Enjoying the cashew horchata after a day of consuming other juices feels like an immense treat. I think you will agree when you try it. Note: If you don't have a high-speed blender, soak your cashews and dates in the 2 cups water in a pint mason jar for 2 to 4 hours before blending.

2 tablespoons raw cashew pieces, or whole cashews, roughly chopped
2 to 4 soft medjool dates, pitted and snipped into bits
2 cups filtered water
1/2 teaspoon ground cinnamon

In a blender, combine the cashews, dates, water, and cinnamon. Blend the ingredients until completely smooth and creamy, about 2 minutes.

Optional variations: for more flavor, consider adding any or all of the following: a tiny pinch of salt, 1 teaspoon of Mexican vanilla extract, or a drop of therapeutic-grade cinnamon essential oil for more intense cinnamon flavor.

Press all of your fruits and vegetables through your juicer. Strain the juice if desired. Juice is best stored in lidded glass jars.

MAKES ABOUT 64 OUNCES (4 PINTS)

Part 4

Fitness and

Maintenance

FOURTEEN

The Fitness Side of Health

WHILE WEIGHT LOSS CAN almost certainly be achieved through diet alone, exercise is pivotal for creating a truly healthy and fit body inside and out. Exercise gives you the additional benefit of burning calories, which makes dieting more effective and more likely to stick. Physical fitness also provides you with feel-good endorphins, strengthens your muscles and your bones, and wards off many illnesses and diseases.

Whether you already have a love affair with fitness or you feel like going to the gym is worse than pulling teeth, the information in this chapter can benefit you, your waistline, and your cardiovascular condition.

America's Growing Obesity Epidemic

Getting the right information about how to achieve health and fitness today is like navigating a confusing maze of information. Choosing a diet and exercise plan is no small task. Weight loss is a $20 billion dollar industry, with more than 100 million people on diets in the United States alone. Fads pop up seemingly every week, each one making lofty promises to help you burn body fat and calories at astonishing rates, lose weight rapidly, and make you look amazing, all while eating your favorite foods.

These programs and fads may or may not be capable of delivering the results you are looking for, but in reality, most of the claims offered by the health and fitness industry are too good to be true. This is partly why most diet products, exercise equipment, and fitness DVDs end up collecting dust in a corner of the attic. Yet the majority of our nation is still overweight. In fact, the percentage of those who are overweight or obese in America has more than doubled in the last thirty years. It is estimated that more than 68 percent of adults are overweight, with nearly half of that number being obese.

So, what's causing this fat epidemic? The short answer is that people are simply eating more food—especially bad food—and moving less. In fact, the average person consumes about 500 more calories per day than in the 1970s and is burning 120 to 140 calories less per day, mostly because of physical inactivity. This combination of overeating and under-exercising is causing us to get fatter. According to the Centers for Disease Control and Prevention, the rising rates of childhood obesity are even more alarming than the rates for adults: they've more than tripled in the last thirty years. For the first time in the last two centuries, it's projected that the next generation of children will live shorter, lower-quality lives than their parents, because of health complications from being overweight or obese.

The Cost of the Nation's Big Fat Crises

Reuters reports that the epidemic is costing our country $190 billion dollars a year in health care dollars. But besides the medical cost involved, being overweight and obese has many other implications. The physical, socioeconomic, and emotional side effects of packing on extra pounds include, but are not limited to, the following: high blood pressure, blood clots, stroke, diabetes, heart disease, joint problems, osteoarthritis, sleep apnea, difficulty sleeping, all kinds of cancers, metabolic syndromes, elevated cholesterol, liver and gall bladder disease, infertility, asthma, discrimination, lower wages, depression, and relationship issues.

A Ridiculously Simple Solution

The craziest part about the overweight/obesity epidemic is that it is entirely preventable and completely reversible. The solution to the problem really is just this: people simply need to eat better and move more. This is the most fundamental and useful keys to successful and sustained weight loss.

The food lifestyle, recipes, and meal plans presented in this book will help you to achieve the eating part of your diet, which experts say is up to 75 percent of the weight-loss solution. However, many people struggle with committing to a daily exercise routine. This chapter is designed to help you achieve the other 25 percent of the equation.

Commit to Just 30 to 45 Minutes a Day

Although it would be ideal to get 60 minutes or more of exercising on a daily basis, getting your body moving even for 30 to 45 minutes every day can help make a significant impact on your overall health and weight. The Mayo Clinic reports that benefits from being active for even a half an hour each day include but are not limited to weight loss, increased stamina, reduced illness, reduced risk of cancer, reduced risk of strokes, reduction in chronic conditions, reduced high blood pressure, reduced incidence in complications of diabetes and coronary artery disease, strengthening of the heart, clearer arteries, decreased depression, reduced anxiety, improved mood, improved mobility and mental clarity while aging, and increased life span. Those are benefits that cannot be met with any prescription or over-the-counter drug or supplement.

Everyone can make time for that amount of exercise on a daily basis. If fitting in that amount of exercise all at once doesn't work for you, break it into 10 minutes 3 to 4 times a day or 15 minutes three times a day for the same benefit.

A Fitness Plan for You

The ideal situation for fitness is to include some form of cardiovascular exercise and some form of strength training on a daily basis. You can join a gym to get the equipment and benefits you need, or you can do everything at home. For home exercise, all you generally need are a good pair of shoes and a small set of free weights. It really doesn't take much to get started—what's really important is taking that first step.

The wonderful thing about exercise is that you can tailor-make your exercise plan. There is literally a type of exercise for each of us. You might even already be doing one or more activities that you can increase, or you can begin a "program" that you are bound to enjoy. Consider this as a very non-comprehensive list of exercises: running, walking, jogging, biking, dancing, kickboxing, aerobics, Pilates, yoga, strength training, tennis, football, basketball, soccer, golf (without a cart), hockey, lacrosse, boxing, martial arts, karate, racquetball, squash, Zumba, CrossFit, walking the dog, taking the stairs, t'ai chi, spinning, swimming, cross country skiing, rebounder, jump rope, skateboarding, surfing, household chores (yes, really!), group fitness classes, snowboarding, equipment cardio, snowshoeing, rock climbing, kayaking, rowing, hiking, and ice skating.

Suggested Exercise Schedule							
	Monday	Tuesday	Wednesday	Thursday	Friday	Saturday	Sunday
CARDIO	30 minutes elliptical training	30 minutes spinning intervals	30 minutes incline treadmill	30 minutes recumbent bike	30 minutes swimming/pool/running	60 minutes restorative yoga	30 minutes walking
STRENGTH	15 minutes upper body strength training	15 minutes Lower body strength training	15 minutes upper body strength training	15 minutes lower body strength training	15 minutes upper body strength training	no strength training	15 minutes Pilates

There's an ongoing debate in the fitness community about whether cardiovascular exercise or strength training is the best way to achieve the right level of fitness. I have found that I perform and look my best when I do a bit of both nearly every single day. That way, my muscles stay toned and my heart and lungs stay strong and healthy.

The most important thing is that you find a way to move your body that makes you happy. Choose the type of exercise that is best for you. An exercise week for you might look very different from one for me, but here is my typical one-week workout plan. You can create your own weekly exercise calendar similar to the one above, based on the activities you enjoy most. It's a good idea to switch up exercises to keep different muscle groups active.

Ten Tips for Gaining or Maintaining Motivation:

The key to finding a happy relationship with exercise is finding fitness motivation. Once you start exercising, those endorphins kick in and it's easier to maintain the desire to work out because you know how good it feels. If you've taken a break from exercise, are recovering from an injury, or have simply gotten bored with your current routine, here are some motivation tips to help you get started again.

1. Music gets you in the groove to exercise. Use your smart phone or portable music player and put together an awesome high-energy playlist with your favorite tunes. Listening to music while exercising can increase your desire to move, provide you with a distraction, improve your performance, reduce your perceived exertion, increase your endurance, and make exercising a much more positive experience. When I don't work out with music, I'm often more sloppy and unmotivated, but when I get the tunes going, I turn into the Energizer bunny, and exercise becomes much more enjoyable while I rock out. Keep the volume in check, though: if exercising outside, you want to be able to hear your surroundings; and at the gym, nobody wants to hear your tunes above their own. Remember to keep your music player charged. There is nothing like being in the middle of a workout and having your battery die.

2. Invest in comfortable workout clothing that fits your body. If you are okay with working out in an old pair of sweatpants and a t-shirt, that's great, but proper workout clothes wick and absorb sweat, reduce chafing, and are generally flattering, which in turn helps you feel better about yourself and more motivated to be confident while you work out.

3. Start slowly. If you haven't been exercising, don't start out by flat-out running or sprinting and lifting more weight than you can handle. Instead, use this example: if you plan to run, start with walking and work your way up to walk-run intervals. Get to a point where you can talk comfortably while jogging, then increase your speed and length of time from there. A general rule for avoiding injury is to increase your distance no more than 10 percent per week. Apply that rule to strength training as well, with the amount of pounds you lift, to avoid injury.

4. Get outdoors. If the majority of your exercise routine is indoors and you are finding yourself feeling unmotivated, there's nothing like being out in nature to help you rejuvenate. Exercising outside in any weather with the right gear can be comfortable, and help you feel more human and more connected with the earth.

5. Stay hydrated. A good rule of thumb is 8 ounces of water for every 15 minutes of exercise to fend off dehydration. For more vigorous exercise, or if you sweat excessively, increase that amount of water to 8 ounces every 10 minutes.

6. Find a friend. If you have had trouble in the past sticking with exercise, you will greatly improve your odds of showing up and completing the activity if you know that your buddy is counting on you to be there. Without someone relying on you, you are more likely to push the snooze alarm and skip your workout altogether. Workout buddies, especially for women who exercise outside, are good for the old safety-in-numbers rule.

7. Even if you don't feel like going out, get up, get your workout clothes on, and lace up those exercise shoes. Finding time for fitness makes you more positive and happy, and I promise that you will rarely (if ever) regret working out; whereas skipping out will likely make you feel slothful.

8. Commit to a time and stick to it. Exercising first thing in the morning is best for most people because it's out of the way before most of the rest of the world even gets out of bed. I'm not saying you have to get up before the crack of dawn, but exercise later in the day has a way of ending up on the back burner when something else gets in the way and throws you off track. If lunchtime, afternoon, or even evening works better for you because of your schedule, make sure your time is blocked out specifically for that purpose.

9. Find a realistic fitness hero to emulate, with a body type that is achievable for your size and frame. This can be somebody famous, a friend or family member whom you admire, or even your previously fit self. Display an image of that person somewhere you'll see it every day as a reminder of the goal that you want to achieve.

10. Set realistic fitness goals and have fun. No, really—when I get too serious about exercise is when I stop enjoying it. If I set my expectations too high and fail to achieve my goals, I am more miserable than if I hadn't tried in the first place. Enjoy the process, and you'll be much more likely to stick with it in the long term.

FIFTEEN

Success Beyond 28 Days

ONE OF THE QUESTIONS I WAS ASKED the most on my website during my original Green Smoothie Challenge, was if the results from the plan would result in a permanent weight loss. You may be wondering the same thing: how to maintain your new diet and waistline after you finish *The Abundance Diet* plan.

If you were eating unhealthily before beginning this plan and not exercising and you go back to that way of life, you will most likely gradually regain all the weight you lost and lose the health benefits that you developed in the 28 days. So, how do you keep it up? And if you need to continue to lose weight beyond the 28 days, what do you need to do next?

My first piece of advice to you, no matter where you are at, is to keep practicing self-love and nourishing your body with the right foods. This means that you get to keep eating multiple meals a day and to continue an "Eat-on-Repeat" calories or program without counting points. This method, as you've learned, will help save you time on food preparation, save you money, and reduce the amount of food waste in your kitchen. Also, having a well-planned food agenda is the key to successfully keeping your newfound figure or to continue working towards the one you want.

If you have reached your goal weight or size, a modified maintenance diet based mostly on *The Abundance Diet,* along with a properly planned exercise regimen, will likely be enough to keep you on track. Some people refer to this as an 80/20 plan, meaning that, if you eat very healthily 80 percent of the time, some indulgence here and there won't likely hurt your progress unless you overdo negative food choices. Strict adherence isn't necessary, but you just want to make sure you are eating a diet largely based on fresh produce, legumes, whole grains, nuts and seeds. If you begin to see the scale slide back up, or if your jeans get too tight, it may be time for a quick reboot of the program.

For those of you following this plan who desire continued weight loss, you can simply repeat the program for as long as you need to get the desired amount of weight off. There are plenty of recipes in the book that are not used in the 4-week meal plan which you can rotate through to keep your food choices from getting boring. You can also get creative and invent your own recipes based on the food principles taught in this book. Be sure to continue to exercise on a daily basis and stick with the food plan as much as possible. The highest level of success is usually only achieved through consistency.

You may find it necessary to search out restaurants with decent and healthy plant-based options. Not all of us can prepare our meals from scratch all the time, nor is it fun to do so! You might be surprised at the options out there. Ethnic restaurants are often a good choice if you stick largely to plant-based meals served with healthful salads and that are not drenched in oil. Call before you eat out if you find it difficult to get the kind of meal you are after. Chefs and restaurant staff are often far more accommodating than you might think. Voting with those choices also helps restaurants provide more healthy and vegan options as the demand grows.

Don't get discouraged if you make poor food choices. Beware of spirals in which you eat one thing that isn't good for you, so you just keep eating because you get caught in a negative trap.

It's easy to give in every once in a while and indulge in a food that may be calorie-dense and nutrient-poor. When you do, enjoy the food. Savor it and make it mean something, then simply move on. Too many people rebuke themselves over food choices, which then reignites a negative cycle of yo-yo dieting, extreme calorie counting, overeating, or shame-eating. So don't allow mishaps to make you feel discouraged; simply recommit to your health and move forward.

It is my hope that, on this journey, you will gain more than you will have lost in the development compassion for yourself and for animals. You can truly find peace through conscientious eating and living when you are doing it for the right reasons.

Acknowledgments

So much gratitude and thanks to my recipe testers who helped make this book a reality. Your kitchen expertise helped to improve so many of the recipes and there are nuances of each of you found throughout. When we started this journey together, I had no idea that we would form such close and beautiful friendships, I love each and every one of you! Poppy Velosa, Susan, Terri Cole, Jenn Keohane, Monika Soria Caruso, Tami Kramer, Elizabeth Thompson, Shereen Salah, Eve Lynch, Heather Talbot Winkler, Cintia Bock, Kathryn Piovesan, Amy Noffsinger, Hunter Noffsinger, Debby Kastner, Erin Scharr, Megan Toombs, Amanda Williams, Erika Oberle Qureshi, Larry Adams, Stephanie Thayer and Nikki.

A huge and heartfelt thanks to Annie Oliverio, who has been one of my closest friends since the beginning of my vegan journey. For testing and retesting countless recipes, creating the stunning photography and cover art for this book and so much more. This book wouldn't have been possible without you.

Additional thanks to Robin Robertson for professional advice concerning portions of this book and to Jon Roberston and the staff at Vegan Heritage Press for their insight, patience and kindness toward me while I wrote this book over the course of two years while juggling an accident, surgery, physical therapy, recovery and motherhood and more.

All the love to my huge McCowan Clan: Boni, Milo, Wendy, Holly, James, Michelle, Clint, Ben, Abe, and Morgan.

And finally, loving thanks to my biggest supporters, my husband, children, and my dog. You drank all my crazy smoothie combos, helped me come up with the names for the recipes and put up with me during all the late nights while putting this project together. I'm so lucky to have you.

Bibliography

Campbell, T. Colin, and Thomas M. Campbell. *The China Study: The Most Comprehensive Study of Nutrition Ever Conducted and the Startling Implications for Diet, Weight Loss and Long-term Health.* Dallas, TX: BenBella, 2005.

Esselstyn, Caldwell, B. M. D. *Prevent and Reverse Heart Disease.* New York: Penguin Group, 2007.

Fuhrman, Joel. *Super Immunity: The Essential Nutrition Guide for Boosting Your Body's Defenses to Live Longer, Stronger, and Disease Free.* New York: HarperOne, 2011.

About the Author

Somer McCowan has been cooking since her teens and has a passion for experimenting with food and inventing delicious recipes. She has worked in the food industry in the United States and Australia, creating food in bakeries, several restaurants, and a juice bar.

Several years ago, after being diagnosed with a severe autoimmune disease, she was put on multiple prescription drugs and felt terrible. She then discovered that a whole foods, plant-based diet can reverse disease. Somer then went completely vegan and she is now off all prescription drugs and in full remission. Somer loves helping others improve their health through eating the right kinds of food. Her food blog is: www.vedgedout.com.

Instagram: www.instagram.com/somermccowan

Twitter: www.twitter.com/vedgedout

Facebook: www.facebook.com/pages/Vedged-Out

Linked In: www.linkedin.com/pub/somer-mccowan

Index

Metric Conversions and Equivalents

The recipes in this book have not been tested with metric measurements, so some variations may occur.

LIQUID	
U.S.	METRIC
1 tsp	5 ml
1 tbs	15 ml
2 tbs	30 ml
1/4 cup	60 ml
1/3 cup	75 ml
1/2 cup	120 ml
2/3 cup	150 ml
3/4 cup	180 ml
1 cup	240 ml
1 1/4 cups	300 ml
1 1/3 cups	325 ml
1 1/2 cups	350 ml
1 2/3 cups	375 ml
1 3/4 cups	400 ml
2 cups (1 pint)	475 ml
3 cups	720 ml
4 cups (1 quart)	945 ml

GENERAL METRIC CONVERSION FORMULAS	
Ounces to grams	ounces x 28.35 = grams
Grams to ounces	grams x 0.035 = ounces
Pounds to grams	pounds x 435.5 = grams
Pounds to kilograms	pounds x 0.45 = kilograms
Cups to liters	cups x 0.24 = liters
Fahrenheit to Celsius	$(°F - 32) \times 5 \div 9 = °C$
Celsius to Fahrenheit	$(°C \times 9) \div 5 + 32 = °F$

WEIGHT	
U.S.	METRIC
1/2 oz	14 g
1 oz	28 g
1 1/2 oz	43 g
2 oz	57 g
2 1/2 oz	71 g
4 oz	113 g
5 oz	142 g
6 oz	170 g
7 oz	200 g
8 oz (1/2 lb)	227 g
9 oz	255 g
10 oz	284 g
11 oz	312 g
12 oz	340 g
13 oz	368 g
14 oz	400 g
15 oz	425 g
16 oz (1 lb)	454 g

OVEN TEMPERATURE		
°F	Gas Mark	°C
250	1/2	120
275	1	140
300	2	150
325	3	165
350	4	180
375	5	190
400	6	200
425	7	220
450	8	230
475	9	240
500	10	260
550	Broil	290

LENGTH	
U.S.	Metric
1/2 inch	1.25 cm
1 inch	2.5 cm
6 inches	15 cm
8 inches	20 cm
10 inches	25 cm
12 inches	30 cm